YOU SAY YOU WANT TO SAVE THE PLANET

You Say You Want to Save the Planet

Do You Know What it Will Take

JOHN H. SWINFORD III

IngramSpark

CONTENTS

Acknowledgements

Publisher: IngramSparks

Influencers:

The Tuscarora Reservation, Niagara County, New York.

My Mother – Teaching me what is important in life.

Contributor: ChatGPT Artificial Intelligence

Scientist world-wide believe, that limiting global warming beyond 1.5 degrees Celsius (°C) compared to pre-industrial levels is a critical target outlined in the Paris Agreement, as exceeding this threshold would have severe and potentially irreversible impacts on the planet. Yet policies currently in place point to a 2.8°C temperature rise by the end of the century.

The science is clear; our climate is heating rapidly. The average global temperatures have increased by approximately 1.1 degrees Celsius since 1880s, particularly in the late 19th century. The concentration of atmospheric CO_2 is at its highest level ever. The Intergovernmental Panel on Climate Change (IPCC) steadily points out that human activities have warmed the atmosphere, ocean, and land, producing widespread and rapid changes in the atmosphere, ocean, cryosphere, and biosphere. Due to these changes in climate, the number of weather, climate and water-related disasters has increased by a factor of five over the past 50 years. In the United States alone, this has contributed to over 2 million deaths and $3.64 trillion in losses.[3]

The warming is not uniform across all regions and seasons, but the overall trend indicates a significant and sustained increase. It is important to note that year-to-year fluctuations and regional variations can occur, but the long-term trend clearly shows an upward trajectory in global temperatures.

The consequences of this warming trend are diverse

and include more frequent and severe heatwaves, changes in precipitation patterns, rising sea levels, loss of polar ice, shifts in ecosystems and species distribution, and other climate-related impacts. Monitoring and understanding these temperature changes are crucial for developing effective strategies to mitigate and adapt to the impacts of global warming. Scientists, organizations, and governments worldwide continue to study and analyze temperature data to inform policies and actions aimed at addressing climate change and reducing greenhouse gas emissions.

While there may be individuals who argue that the planet does not need saving, it is important to consider the overwhelming scientific consensus and evidence that supports the urgent need for environmental conservation and sustainable practices. Despite the existence of disinformation, the scientific consensus maintains that global warming is real, primarily caused by human activities, and poses significant risks to the planet and its inhabitants.

The goal of this book is to help individuals develop critical thinking skills that are essential to discern reliable information from misinformation, ultimately increasing awareness and Global Citizenship. I hope to arm future generations with critical thinking capabilities, and knowledge for protecting our planet, while eliminating urban legends and meths. This is a book based off my research and opinions.

~ 1 ~

NATIVE AMERICAN'S LOVE FOR THE PLANET

Native Americans have a deep spiritual connection to the planet and view the Earth as a living, sacred entity. Their spiritual beliefs often center around the interconnectedness of all beings and the recognition of the Earth as a provider of life and sustenance.

Many Native American tribes hold the belief that the Earth is their mother and that all living beings, including humans, animals, plants, and natural elements, are part of one interconnected web of life. This perspective fosters a sense of respect, gratitude, and responsibility towards the Earth and its natural resources.

Native American spiritual practices often involve rituals and ceremonies that honor and connect with the Earth. These practices vary among tribes and may include offerings, prayers, dances, songs, and storytelling. Through these rituals, individuals seek to establish harmony and balance with nature, as well as to express gratitude for the Earth's gifts.

The natural elements, such as water, air, fire, and earth, hold significant spiritual importance in many Native American traditions. They are seen as sources of life and symbols of purification, transformation, and renewal. Native Americans often engage in specific ceremonies and rituals to honor and seek guidance from these elements.

Overall, the spiritual connection that Native Americans have with the planet is rooted in a deep reverence for the Earth and an understanding of humanity's interdependence with the natural world. It is a profound relationship that encompasses both respect for the Earth's resources and a responsibility to care for and protect them for future generations.

~ 2 ~

URBAN LEGENDS

Economics Teacher: Bueller? Bueller? Bueller?

Simone: Um, he's sick. My best friend's sister's boyfriend's brother's girlfriend heard from this guy who knows this kid who's going with the girl who saw Ferris pass out at 31 Flavors last night. I guess it's pretty serious.

Urban legends are often based on exaggerated or fictional stories that circulate widely within a society. While there may be urban legends related to saving the planet, it's important to approach them with skepticism and verify information using credible sources. Here are a few examples of urban legends that have been associated with environmental conservation:

"Using a single paper straw saves a turtle": This urban legend suggests that switching from plastic to paper straws can directly save the lives of marine animals like turtles. While reducing plastic waste is indeed beneficial for the environment, the specific impact of a single straw on marine life is exaggerated. Plastic pollution remains a significant threat to marine ecosystems, but the focus should be on systemic changes and comprehensive waste management rather than individual actions.

"Turning off one light bulb can save the planet": This legend implies that conserving energy by turning off a single light bulb can have a massive impact on global energy consumption and environmental preservation. While energy conservation is important, it requires collective efforts and systemic changes beyond the actions of a single light bulb. It is crucial to adopt energy-efficient practices in all areas of life and promote sustainable energy sources.

"Planting a single tree offsets your carbon footprint": This legend suggests that planting a single tree can fully offset an individual's carbon footprint and negate the environmental impact of their actions. While trees play a vital role in carbon sequestration and ecosystem health, the extent to which a single tree can offset carbon emissions is exaggerated. Addressing climate change requires a comprehensive approach, including reducing emissions, transitioning to renewable energy, and protecting and restoring forests.

"Recycling is always better than throwing away":

This legend implies that all recycling efforts are equally effective in reducing waste and protecting the environment. While recycling is crucial, it is not a foolproof solution. The effectiveness of recycling depends on various factors, including proper sorting, recycling infrastructure, market demand for recycled materials, and consumer behavior. Reducing waste at the source and promoting a circular economy approach that prioritizes reuse and reduction should be emphasized alongside recycling.

It is important to critically evaluate information and rely on reputable sources such as scientific research, government agencies, and established environmental organizations when it comes to understanding the most effective ways to address environmental challenges. By relying on accurate information, we can make informed decisions and contribute meaningfully to the preservation of our planet.

When it comes to weather changes and climate changes, there are a few urban legends or misconceptions that have circulated. It's important to note that these claims are not scientifically supported or are misinterpretations of the complex relationship between climate change and weather patterns. Here are a couple of examples:

"Climate change causes extreme weather events like hurricanes and tornadoes to become more frequent and intense in all regions": While climate change can influence weather patterns, it is incorrect to attribute individual weather events solely to climate change. Weather events like hurricanes, tornadoes, and storms have natural variability and are influenced by various factors beyond climate change, such as atmospheric conditions and local geography. Climate change can contribute to the intensity and frequency of some extreme weather events, but the specific impacts vary by region and require careful analysis.

"Cold weather or snowstorms disprove the existence of climate change": This urban legend suggests that cold weather events or snowstorms contradict the idea of global warming or climate change. However, weather patterns and climate change are distinct phenomena. Climate change refers to long-term shifts in average temperature and weather patterns over an extended period, while weather events are short-term and can vary widely. Cold weather events can still occur within a changing climate, and localized weather conditions do not negate the overall trend of global warming observed over decades.

It's essential to rely on scientific research and expert consensus to understand the complex relationship between climate change and weather patterns. While climate change can influence weather systems and increase the likelihood of certain extreme events, attributing individual weather events solely to climate change is often misleading. The focus should be on long-term trends and the overall impact of climate change on the Earth's climate system.

Urban legends related to climate change can perpetuate misinformation or misconceptions about the causes, impacts, and solutions of climate change. It's important to rely on scientifically supported information when discussing climate change. Here are a few examples of urban legends associated with climate change:

"Climate change is a natural cycle, and human activities have no influence": This urban legend suggests that climate change is solely driven by natural processes and that human activities have no impact on the Earth's climate system. However, extensive scientific evidence indicates that human activities, particularly the burning of fossil fuels and deforestation, are major contributors to the increased concentration of greenhouse gases in the atmosphere, leading to global warming.

"Climate change is a hoax or conspiracy": This legend suggests that climate change is a fabricated concept or a result of a global conspiracy. However, the overwhelming consensus among scientists and international organizations is that climate change is real, primarily caused by human activities, and poses significant risks to the planet and its inhabitants. Multiple lines of evidence, including temperature records, melting ice caps, and changing weather patterns, support the scientific consensus on climate change.

"Climate change will only bring positive effects, such as longer growing seasons": This urban legend presents a distorted view of climate change by suggesting that it will bring only positive outcomes. While it is true that certain regions may experience longer growing seasons or milder winters, climate change also poses significant risks and challenges. These include extreme weather events, sea-level rise, habitat loss, and disruptions to ecosystems and livelihoods. The negative impacts of climate change far outweigh any potential benefits.

"Climate change can be stopped completely if we just reduce carbon emissions": This legend oversimplifies the complex nature of climate change. While reducing greenhouse gas emissions is essential to mitigate climate change, achieving complete eradication is challenging due to the long-lived nature of greenhouse gases and existing atmospheric concentrations. Climate change requires a multifaceted approach that includes adaptation strategies, sustainable development practices, and global cooperation to limit its impacts.

"Climate change is solely responsible for extreme weather events": This urban legend suggests that every individual extreme weather event can be directly attributed to climate change. While climate change can influence the frequency and intensity of certain extreme events, attributing specific weather events solely to climate change is scientifically challenging. Weather patterns are influenced by a range of factors, including natural variability. However, the overall trend of increasing extreme weather events aligns with climate change projections.

It is important to rely on credible sources, scientific research, and consensus from reputable scientific institutions when discussing climate change. Engaging in informed discussions helps ensure accurate understanding and effective action towards addressing the challenges posed by climate change.

While there may be various urban legends or misconceptions surrounding the health and condition of the planet, it's important to rely on accurate information and scientific consensus. Here are a few examples of urban legends associated with the belief that the planet is dying:

"The Earth will be destroyed by an imminent apocalypse": This legend suggests that the planet is on the brink of imminent destruction, often attributed to a specific event or catastrophe. However, while there are environmental challenges and risks to address, the notion of an impending total destruction of the planet is not supported by scientific evidence. It is crucial to focus on sustainable practices and collective efforts to address environmental issues.

"The Earth is running out of resources, and we're

doomed": This legend implies that the planet's resources are depleting rapidly, leading to an inevitable collapse of civilization. While resource management and sustainability are important, the notion that the Earth is running out of resources in a way that will cause a catastrophic collapse is an oversimplification. Responsible resource management, innovation, and transitioning to sustainable practices can help ensure a more sustainable future.

"The planet is dying, and there's nothing we can do about it": This legend perpetuates a sense of helplessness and resignation, suggesting that environmental degradation is irreversible and inevitable. While there are pressing environmental challenges, it is important to recognize that human actions have the potential to make a positive difference. By adopting sustainable practices, conservation efforts, and advocating for responsible policies, individuals and communities can contribute to a healthier planet.

"There is no hope for the planet's recovery": This legend claims that the planet's condition is beyond repair or recovery, leading to a sense of hopelessness. However, there are numerous successful environmental conservation and restoration efforts taking place globally. It is important to acknowledge and support these initiatives, as they demonstrate that positive change is possible when we take collective action.

There are some who believe that weather is circular. Weather is not circular. Weather patterns and conditions do not follow a circular or cyclical path. Weather is influenced by various factors, including atmospheric pressure systems, temperature gradients, moisture content, and the Earth's rotation. These factors interact in complex ways, leading to the formation of weather patterns and the occurrence of different weather conditions.

Weather patterns can vary greatly from one location to another and can change rapidly over short time periods. They can exhibit a wide range of patterns, such as high or low-pressure systems, fronts, cyclones, anticyclones, and various types of precipitation. These patterns are not circular in nature but are influenced by the dynamic and constantly changing interactions of atmospheric processes.

While certain weather phenomena, such as the seasons, can follow cyclical patterns, the day-to-day weather conditions are not circular. They are determined by the dynamic and often chaotic behavior of the atmosphere, which can result in a wide variety of weather patterns and conditions.

There are others who believe that weather is independent of climate change.

Weather: Weather refers to the atmospheric conditions in a specific place at a particular time, such as temperature, precipitation, wind speed, and humidity.

It includes daily or short-term variations in these conditions.

Climate Change: Climate change refers to long-term changes in average weather patterns and conditions over a significant period, typically decades to centuries. It is primarily driven by factors like human activities (such as greenhouse gas emissions) and natural processes, resulting in shifts in temperature, precipitation patterns, sea level rise, and other climatic variables.

Given these definitions, weather and climate change are distinct but interconnected concepts. Weather conditions can vary on a daily or even hourly basis, while climate change refers to longer-term trends and shifts in climate patterns.

While individual weather events (such as a single storm or a hot day) cannot be directly attributed to climate change, scientists have found that climate change can influence and exacerbate certain weather phenomena. For example, it can contribute to more intense heatwaves, heavier rainfall events, or stronger hurricanes. Climate change impacts are observed over extended periods, and their effects become more apparent when examining long-term trends and statistical analyses of weather patterns.

So, weather and climate change are not independent of each other. Weather represents short-term variations, while climate change refers to long-term shifts in weather patterns and conditions.

It is essential to seek accurate information from reputable scientific sources, organizations, and experts when discussing the health of the planet. While there are significant environmental challenges, it is important to remain informed, engage in sustainable practices, support conservation efforts, and work towards solutions to preserve and protect our planet for future generations.

$$\sim 3 \sim$$

WHO ARE WE TRYING TO PROTECT, BY PROTECTING THE PLANET

By protecting the planet, we aim to safeguard the well-being and interests of various stakeholders, including:

Future Generations: Protecting the planet is crucial for the well-being of future generations. By taking care of the environment, we ensure that they have access to clean air, water, and resources necessary for their survival and development.

Human Society: A healthy planet is essential for the overall well-being and quality of life of human society. Protecting the environment helps to mitigate the impacts of climate change, reduce pollution, preserve ecosystems, and promote sustainable development, which in turn benefits human health, livelihoods, and social stability.

Biodiversity and Ecosystems: The planet is home to an incredible diversity of species and ecosystems, which provide essential ecological services such as pollination, water purification, climate regulation, and nutrient cycling. Protecting the environment helps preserve biodiversity and ensures the functioning of these ecosystems, benefiting both wildlife and humans.

Indigenous Peoples and Local Communities: Indigenous peoples and local communities often have deep cultural, spiritual, and economic connections with their surrounding environments. Protecting the planet involves respecting their rights, knowledge, and traditional practices, as well as ensuring their sustainable livelihoods and cultural preservation.

Vulnerable Populations: The impacts of environmental degradation, climate change, and pollution often disproportionately affect vulnerable populations, including low-income communities, marginalized groups, and developing nations. By protecting the planet, we strive to reduce these inequalities and promote environmental justice.

Global Stability and Security: Environmental issues, such as climate change, deforestation, and resource scarcity, can have far-reaching implications for global stability and security. Protecting the planet helps mitigate conflicts over natural resources, reduce displacement and migration, and foster international cooperation for sustainable development.

Ultimately, by protecting the planet, we safeguard the intricate web of life, support human well-being, and ensure a sustainable future for all living beings. It is a collective responsibility that transcends borders, cultures, and generations. Let's define some of the above to ensure we are on the same page and understanding.

Biodiversity refers to the variety of life forms found on Earth, including plants, animals, fungi, and microorganisms, as well as the ecological processes and interactions that sustain them. It encompasses the richness and variety of genes, species, and ecosystems that exist in different habitats and ecosystems around the world.

Ecosystems, on the other hand, are dynamic and interconnected systems formed by living organisms and their surrounding physical environment. They consist of a community of organisms (including plants, animals, and microorganisms) interacting with each other and with the non-living components of their environment, such as air, water, soil, and sunlight. Ecosystems can range from small-scale habitats, like a pond or a forest, to large-scale systems, such as a coral reef or a tropical rainforest.

Biodiversity and ecosystems are closely intertwined. Ecosystems rely on biodiversity to function and provide important services to both nature and humans. These services, often referred to as ecosystem services, include:

Provisioning Services: Ecosystems provide resources essential for human survival, such as food, fresh water, timber, fiber, and medicinal plants.

Regulating Services: Ecosystems regulate important processes in the environment, such as climate regulation, water purification, soil fertility, and natural hazard mitigation.

Supporting Services: Biodiversity within ecosystems supports critical processes, such as nutrient cycling, pollination, seed dispersal, and decomposition, which are vital for ecosystem functioning and productivity.

Cultural Services: Ecosystems and biodiversity have cultural and aesthetic value, providing recreational opportunities, inspiration for art and literature, and spiritual and cultural significance to communities.

Biodiversity and ecosystems face numerous threats, including habitat destruction, climate change, pollution, overexploitation of resources, invasive species, and fragmentation of habitats. The loss of biodiversity and degradation of ecosystems can have far-reaching consequences, leading to the loss of species, reduced ecosystem resilience, and a decline in the provision of ecosystem services.

Conserving biodiversity and protecting ecosystems is crucial for maintaining the health of the planet and ensuring sustainable development. It involves preserving habitats, preventing species extinctions, promoting sustainable land and resource management practices, and fostering awareness and understanding of the value of biodiversity and ecosystems among individuals, communities, and decision-makers.

~ 4 ~

THE ARGUMENTS OVER SAVING OUR PLANET

The topic of saving the planet encompasses a wide range of arguments and perspectives. Here are some common arguments related to the importance of environmental conservation and sustainability:

Environmental Stewardship: Supporters of saving the planet argue that it is our moral and ethical responsibility to protect the environment and preserve the Earth's natural resources for future generations. They emphasize the intrinsic value of nature and the need to maintain ecological balance.

Climate Change Mitigation: The urgency to save the planet is often linked to the need to mitigate climate change. Advocates argue that reducing greenhouse gas emissions and transitioning to renewable energy sources are essential to prevent catastrophic impacts on ecosystems, human health, and the global economy.

Biodiversity Conservation: Supporters emphasize the importance of preserving biodiversity—the variety of plant and animal species—and protecting fragile ecosystems. They argue that maintaining biodiversity is crucial for ecosystem functioning, ecological services (such as pollination and water purification), and the discovery of new medicines and technologies.

Sustainable Development: Advocates for saving the planet argue for a shift towards sustainable development practices. They promote economic growth that considers environmental protection, social equity, and long-term resource management. They believe that sustainable practices can support economic prosperity while minimizing environmental degradation.

Public Health and Well-being: Protecting the planet is seen as integral to human health and well-being. Supporters argue that reducing pollution, improving air and water quality, and promoting sustainable agriculture can lead to healthier populations, lower healthcare costs, and an improved quality of life.

Economic Opportunities: Proponents of environmental conservation argue that investing in renewable energy, clean technologies, and sustainable practices can stimulate economic growth, create jobs, and foster innovation. They believe that transitioning to a green economy can provide long-term economic benefits.

Environmental Justice: The argument for saving the planet often includes considerations of environmental justice and equity. Supporters highlight the disproportionate impacts of environmental degradation and climate change on marginalized communities and advocate for inclusive solutions that address social, economic, and environmental disparities.

It's important to note that saving the planet requires collective action and global cooperation. While there may be differing perspectives on the specific approaches and priorities, the overall objective is to ensure a sustainable future for both the planet and its inhabitants.

THE HEATED TOPIC OF CLIMATE CHANGE

Climate change refers to long-term shifts in temperature patterns and weather conditions on Earth. Climate change is primarily driven by human activities, particularly the release of greenhouse gases into the atmosphere from burning fossil fuels (such as coal, oil, and natural gas), deforestation, and industrial processes. These greenhouse gases trap heat in the Earth's atmosphere, leading to a gradual increase in global temperatures, changes in precipitation patterns, rising sea levels, and other environmental impacts.

Climate change has wide-ranging consequences, including the loss of biodiversity, more frequent and severe weather events (such as hurricanes, heatwaves, and droughts), disruptions to ecosystems, and risks to human health and well-being. Addressing climate change requires global cooperation, reduction in greenhouse gas emissions, transition to renewable energy sources, conservation efforts, and adaptation strategies to mitigate its impacts.

Climate change is a heated topic for several reasons:

Scientific Consensus: The scientific community overwhelmingly agrees that climate change is primarily caused by human activities, particularly the emission of greenhouse gases from burning fossil fuels. However, there are still individuals and groups who deny or dispute this consensus. This disagreement can lead to intense debates and arguments.

Global Impact: Climate change has far-reaching consequences for the planet and all its inhabitants. It affects ecosystems, weather patterns, sea levels, and the availability of resources. The potential risks associated with climate change, such as extreme weather events, displacement of populations, and threats to food security, generate strong emotions and concerns.

Natural Cycles: Some argue that environmental changes and challenges are part of natural cycles and that the Earth has experienced periods of warming, cooling, and other shifts throughout its history. They may claim that the current changes are part of this natural variation, and therefore, there is no need for intervention.

Counterpoint: While the Earth has indeed gone through natural climate variations in the past, the current changes are occurring at an unprecedented rate. The scientific consensus attributes the current climate change primarily to human activities, such as burning fossil fuels and deforestation, which release significant amounts of greenhouse gases into the atmosphere.

Policy Implications: Addressing climate change requires significant changes in energy systems, transportation, agriculture, and other sectors. This can involve policy decisions that impact economies, industries, and individual lifestyles. Disagreements arise regarding the best strategies, costs, and trade-offs involved in mitigating and adapting to climate change.

Technological Solutions: Some individuals believe that advancements in technology will eventually solve any environmental issues that arise. They argue that technological innovations, such as geo-engineering or future breakthroughs, will provide the means to mitigate any potential problems.

Counterpoint: While technological advancements can play a crucial role in addressing environmental challenges, relying solely on future solutions is risky. The current state of the planet demands immediate action to prevent irreversible damage. Moreover, relying solely on unproven or hypothetical technologies to address environmental issues overlooks the fact that many effective and readily available solutions already exist, such as transitioning to renewable energy sources and adopting sustainable practices.

Economic Interests: Certain industries, such as fossil fuel extraction and production, may face significant challenges as the world transitions to a low-carbon economy. There can be conflicting interests between those who advocate for immediate action on climate change and those who are concerned about the economic implications and potential job losses associated with such transitions.

Economic Concerns: Opponents of environmental conservation may argue that prioritizing environmental protection and sustainability comes at the expense of economic growth and development. They may contend that regulations and initiatives aimed at saving the planet place burdens on industries and impede economic progress.

Counterpoint: The long-term costs of environmental degradation, such as health impacts, natural resource depletion, and the consequences of climate change, can have severe economic consequences. Investments in renewable energy, clean technologies, and sustainable practices can actually create new industries, generate jobs, and drive

economic growth while safeguarding the environment.

Political Divides: Climate change is often entangled in political ideologies, with differing views on the role of government, regulations, and international cooperation. Political polarization can hinder progress on climate change as it becomes a divisive issue along party lines.

Short-Term vs. Long-Term Perspectives: Climate change is a long-term problem that requires action today for future benefits. However, short-term priorities, immediate economic gains, and political cycles often take precedence. Balancing short-term concerns with long-term sustainability goals can lead to heated discussions and disagreements.

Media Coverage and Disinformation: The media plays a significant role in shaping public opinion and understanding of climate change. Conflicting narratives, misinformation, and biased reporting can amplify controversies and hinder a nuanced understanding of the issue.

Sensationalism and False Balance: In an effort to attract attention or present "balanced" perspectives, some media outlets may sensationalize climate-related stories or give undue prominence to fringe viewpoints that deny or downplay the scientific consensus on global warming. This false balance can create confusion among the public and lead to the perception of a scientific debate that does not exist.

Selective Reporting: Media outlets may selectively cover climate-related events or focus on specific controversies while neglecting the broader scientific consensus. This selective reporting can skew public understanding by downplaying the overall urgency and significance of global warming.

Influence of Special Interests: Certain media outlets, driven by their financial interests or ideological agendas, may promote disinformation or biased narratives about global warming. Fossil fuel industries, for example, have been known to fund climate denial campaigns and exert influence over media coverage to protect their economic interests.

Lack of Scientific Expertise: Journalists without a solid understanding of climate science may inadvertently misinterpret or misrepresent scientific findings, leading to inaccurate reporting. Complex scientific concepts and uncertainties associated with climate change can be challenging to communicate accurately to the general public.

Social Media and Online Disinformation: The rise of social media platforms has facilitated the spread of disinformation and misinformation on global warming. False or misleading information can quickly go viral, influencing public perceptions and undermining accurate scientific knowledge.

To address these challenges, media literacy and critical thinking skills are essential for the public to discern reliable information from misinformation. Fact-checking organizations and initiatives can help identify and debunk false claims. Additionally, efforts by reputable media outlets to adhere to journalistic standards, provide accurate and balanced reporting, and highlight the overwhelming scientific consensus on global warming are crucial in combatting disinformation.

Given the complex nature of climate change and its wide-ranging implications, it is natural for it to be a heated topic of discussion. It is crucial to approach these discussions with scientific evidence, open-mindedness, and a willingness to find common ground for effective solutions.

$$\sim 6 \sim$$

OUR CHALLENGE

Saving our planet and addressing the environmental challenges we face is a complex and multifaceted task. Here are some of the key challenges that need to be addressed:

Climate Change: Climate change is one of the most pressing global challenges we face. Rising temperatures, extreme weather events, sea-level rise, and other climate impacts are threatening ecosystems, biodiversity, and human well-being. Addressing climate change requires reducing greenhouse gas emissions, transitioning to clean and renewable energy sources, and adapting to the changing climate.

Biodiversity Loss: The loss of biodiversity is a significant concern. Habitat destruction, deforestation, pollution, overfishing, and climate change are causing the extinction of plant and animal species at an alarming rate. Protecting and restoring habitats, implementing sustainable land-use practices, and combating illegal wildlife trade are crucial for preserving biodiversity.

Pollution: Pollution, including air pollution, water pollution, and soil contamination, poses significant risks to human health and ecosystems. Reducing pollution requires stricter regulations, improved waste management systems, cleaner technologies, and increased public awareness about the impacts of pollution.

Resource Depletion: Unsustainable consumption and production patterns are depleting natural resources, including freshwater, minerals, and forests. Transitioning to a circular economy that promotes resource efficiency, recycling, and responsible consumption can help alleviate the strain on finite resources.

Deforestation: Deforestation, primarily driven by agriculture, logging, and urbanization, leads to the loss of vital forest ecosystems and contributes to climate change. Halting deforestation and promoting reforestation efforts are crucial for carbon sequestration, biodiversity conservation, and sustainable land use.

Water Scarcity: Many regions around the world are facing water scarcity and stress due to population growth, climate change, and unsustainable water management practices. Conserving water, improving water efficiency in agriculture, and implementing effective water management strategies are essential for ensuring water availability for all.

Sustainable Agriculture: The current agricultural practices, including intensive farming, excessive use of fertilizers and pesticides, and deforestation for agricultural expansion, have negative environmental impacts. Transitioning to sustainable agriculture practices, such as organic farming, agroecology, and precision farming, can reduce environmental harm while ensuring food security.

Environmental Justice: Environmental challenges disproportionately affect marginalized communities and vulnerable populations. Achieving environmental justice requires addressing social inequalities, ensuring access to clean air, water, and healthy environments for all, and involving communities in decision-making processes.

Addressing these challenges requires collective action, international cooperation, and long-term commitment from governments, businesses, communities, and individuals. It involves adopting sustainable practices, promoting renewable energy, implementing effective policies and regulations, supporting research and innovation, and raising awareness about the importance of protecting our planet for future generations.

~ 7 ~

BRING BACK THE CAMPAIGN COMMERCIALS

Recently I went to a fast-food drive-thru. This restaurant was in a county that banned plastic straws to do their part for the environment. When I pulled up to the window for my order: one soda, burger, and fries, I was handed a paper straw, a large plastic cup with plastic lid, a large drink holder container made from cardboard (for four beverages, when I only order and received one), paper bag with my sandwich rapped in tinfoil, frenchfries in an oversize carboard container, and more napkins than one person could use. Is that one straw making a difference, given all the other items that are impacting our environment? I know, I know, we must start somewhere, and every little bit helps. But, if we are going to do this, let's do it right! Let's start by bringing back the campaign commercials, "Keep America Beautiful."

Many individuals my age can remember the campaign, that started in 1970s, "Keep America Beautiful." One of the earlier commercials showed a Native American canoeing down a river near an industrial complex, smoke bellowing out of the large factories lining the river. There is trash in the water and on the shorelines. It ends with an actor playing the role of a Native American man, getting out of the canoe, and witnessing the pollution and littering caused by modern society. The actor, Iron Eyes Cody, stands and looks directly at the camera as a teardrop runs down his face. Voice overlay narrates, "Some people have a deep abiding respect for the natural beauty that was once this country, and some people don't. People start pollution, people can stop it."[1]

How about the commercial where Iron Eyes Cody is riding a horse through the wood and ends up overlook a Freeway and with trash everywhere. Once again, Iron Eyes Cody turns and looks directly into the camera with a tear running down his face; narration overlay, "The first American people loved the land. They held it in several reverends, and in some Americans today that spirit is reborn. ... People start pollution, people can stop it."[2]

Note: Cody claimed to be of Cherokee Cree descent, although it was later revealed that he was of Italian descent.

What about Woodsy Owl? A fictional character and mascot created for the United States Forest Service. The character was designed to promote environmental conservation and raise awareness about the importance of taking care of forests and natural resources. Woodsy Owl is known for his catchphrase, "Give a hoot! Don't pollute!" and his iconic appearance, which includes a brown owl with a wide-brimmed forest ranger hat and a neckerchief.

Woodsy Owl was first introduced in 1971 as part of a national public service campaign aimed at educating children and adults about environmental issues. The campaign emphasized the importance of preventing pollution, reducing waste, and being responsible stewards of the environment. Woodsy Owl became popular through various educational materials, commercials, and appearances at events.

The character's message focuses on encouraging individuals to make conscious choices that benefit the environment, such as recycling, conserving water, and respecting wildlife. Woodsy Owl's slogan, "Give a hoot, don't pollute!" emphasizes the idea that every person can make a positive impact on the environment by taking simple actions and making environmentally friendly decisions.

Woodsy Owl continues to be recognized and used as a symbol of environmental stewardship in the United States. The character serves as a reminder that protecting and preserving the natural world is a responsibility shared by everyone.

Of course, one of the originals is Smokey the Bear. Smokey Bear is a widely recognized symbol and mascot of wildfire prevention in the United States. He was created in 1944 by the United States Forest Service and the Ad Council to educate the public about the dangers of forest fires and the importance of fire prevention.

The character of Smokey Bear is depicted as a bear wearing a ranger hat and jeans. He is known for his catchphrase, "Only you can prevent forest fires," which has become ingrained in American culture.

Smokey Bear's origins trace back to World War II when the US experienced a shortage of resources due to the war effort. As a result, there was a concern that wildfires caused by human negligence could further strain resources. The Forest Service created the Smokey Bear campaign to raise awareness and encourage individuals to be cautious and responsible when it comes to fire safety.

Over the years, Smokey Bear has appeared in various forms of media, including posters, television commercials, and educational materials, spreading his message of fire prevention. He has become an enduring symbol and a beloved figure in the United States, recognized for his role in promoting responsible behavior and protecting forests from preventable wildfires.

~ 8 ~

THE KEY TO SAVING OUR PLANET

Saving our planet requires addressing several key areas simultaneously. Here are some crucial areas to focus on in efforts to protect and preserve the environment:

Circular economy and waste management: Transitioning to a circular economy model aims to minimize waste generation and promote the efficient use of resources. This involves strategies such as recycling, reusing, and reducing waste, as well as promoting sustainable production and consumption patterns.

Conservation and protection of ecosystems: Preserving biodiversity and protecting ecosystems are critical to maintaining a healthy planet. This involves efforts such as conserving forests, protecting wildlife habitats, promoting sustainable land use practices, and addressing issues like deforestation and habitat destruction.

Sustainable agriculture and food systems: Promoting sustainable agricultural practices can help reduce environmental impacts, such as deforestation, water pollution, and greenhouse gas emissions. Emphasizing organic farming, regenerative agriculture, and reducing food waste are vital components of sustainable food systems.

Water resource management: Protecting and conserving water resources is crucial. Implementing efficient irrigation systems, reducing water pollution, and ensuring access to clean water for all are essential for sustainable development.

Climate change mitigation: Taking immediate action to reduce greenhouse gas emissions is essential. This includes transitioning to renewable energy sources, promoting energy efficiency, adopting sustainable transportation options, and implementing policies to limit carbon emissions from industries.

Environmental education and awareness: Raising awareness and educating individuals about environmental issues is key to driving sustainable behaviors and fostering a sense of responsibility towards the planet. Promoting environmental literacy in schools, communities, and through various media channels can help empower individuals to act.

International cooperation and policy frameworks: Addressing global environmental challenges requires international collaboration. Governments, organizations, and individuals need to work together to develop and implement effective policies, agreements, and frameworks to protect the environment and promote sustainable development.

These are interconnected areas, and progress in one area can positively impact others. It is important for individuals, communities, governments, and businesses to take collective action and adopt sustainable practices in all aspects of life to ensure a better future for our planet and future generations.

~ 9 ~

A CIRCULAR ECONOMY

A circular economy is an economic system aimed at minimizing waste and maximizing the efficient use of resources. It is a departure from the traditional linear "take-make-dispose" model of production and consumption, and instead focuses on creating a closed-loop system where resources are kept in use for as long as possible.

In a circular economy, products and materials are designed, produced, and used in a way that enables them to be reused, repaired, remanufactured, or recycled at the end of their life cycle, rather than being discarded as waste. The goal is to create a regenerative system that reduces resource consumption, minimizes environmental impacts, and fosters sustainable development.

Key principles of a circular economy include:

Design for durability and recyclability: Products are designed to be long-lasting, easily repairable, and made from materials that can be recycled or reused.

Use of renewable energy and sustainable inputs: Renewable energy sources are prioritized, and the use of sustainable raw materials is encouraged to minimize environmental impacts.

Extending product lifespan: Emphasis is placed on maintaining and repairing products to extend their useful life, reducing the need for frequent replacements.

Resource recovery and recycling: Materials from products at the end of their life cycle are recovered, recycled, and reintroduced into the production process, reducing the demand for virgin resources.

Sharing and collaborative consumption: Sharing platforms, such as car-sharing or tool libraries, encourage the utilization of resources by multiple users, reducing the need for individual ownership and minimizing waste.

Reverse logistics and remanufacturing: Efficient collection and recycling systems are established to recover and reintegrate materials and components into new products or to remanufacture them.

Sustainable business models: Companies explore innovative business models, such as product-as-a-service or leasing models, which shift the focus from selling products to providing access to their benefits, encouraging durability and efficient resource use.

Benefits of a circular economy include reduced resource depletion, minimized waste generation, decreased greenhouse gas emissions, increased resource efficiency, job creation, and enhanced resilience to supply chain disruptions.

Transitioning to a circular economy requires collaboration between governments, businesses, and individuals. It involves policy support, innovation, and investment in sustainable infrastructure, as well as changes in consumer behavior and cultural norms to prioritize resource conservation and responsible consumption. Which leads us to conservation and protection of ecosystems.

~ 10 ~

WHEN I WAS GROWING UP

When I was growing up, milk and soda came in class bottles, you paid a deposit for the container. This practice even continued over to soda cans and other beverage and is still practiced in many of the American States. A container deposit, also known as a bottle deposit or beverage container deposit, is a system in which a refundable fee is charged on certain beverage containers at the time of purchase. The deposit is refunded to the consumer when the container is returned for recycling.

Here are some key points about container deposit systems:

Purpose: Container deposit systems aim to promote recycling, reduce litter, and encourage the return and reuse of beverage containers. By providing a financial incentive, these systems motivate consumers to participate in recycling efforts and ensure that containers are properly disposed of.

Eligible Containers: Container deposit systems typically apply to specific types of beverage containers, such as glass bottles, aluminum cans, and plastic bottles. The specific materials and sizes covered can vary depending on the regulations and legislation in each jurisdiction.

Deposit Collection: When purchasing beverages covered by the deposit system, consumers pay an additional amount, which is the deposit fee. This fee is added to the purchase price and is typically listed separately on the receipt. The deposit amount can vary, but it is generally a small portion of the total cost of the beverage.

Return and Refund: Consumers can return the empty beverage containers to designated collection points, such as recycling centers, supermarkets, or reverse vending machines. Once returned, the containers are counted and sorted. Consumers receive a refund equivalent to the deposit amount for each container they return.

Recycling and Reuse: The collected containers are then sent for recycling. Depending on the system, the containers may be processed to create new containers or other products. In some cases, containers are cleaned and sterilized for reuse, reducing the demand for new container production.

Environmental Benefits: Container deposit systems have shown positive environmental impacts. They help to increase recycling rates, reduce litter in public spaces and waterways, conserve resources by reusing materials, and decrease energy consumption and greenhouse gas emissions associated with the production of new containers.

Implementation and Variation: Container deposit systems are implemented and regulated at the regional or national level. The specific details, such as the deposit amount, types of eligible containers, collection infrastructure, and refund processes, can vary from one jurisdiction to another.

It's worth noting that container deposit systems are just one approach to promoting recycling and reducing waste associated with beverage containers. Other waste management strategies, such as curbside recycling programs, may also be in place alongside or instead of container deposit systems, depending on local circumstances and priorities.

WHAT HAPPEN TO BOTTLED MILK AND SODA?

Bottling Milk, refers to the process of packaging fresh milk in bottles for sale and distribution. Over the years, there have been significant changes in the milk industry, including the packaging and distribution of milk. Here are some key developments:

Transition from Glass to Plastic: In the past, milk was commonly bottled in glass containers. However, the industry has gradually shifted towards plastic containers due to their lower cost, lighter weight, and reduced risk of breakage during transportation.

Plastic Milk Jugs: Plastic milk jugs, typically made from high-density polyethylene (HDPE), have become the predominant packaging for milk in many countries. These jugs are lightweight, durable, and easily recyclable. They often feature a plastic screw cap or snap-on lid for convenient opening and closing.

Tetra Pak and Cartons: In addition to plastic jugs, milk is also packaged in cartons made of materials like paperboard, aluminum, and plastic. These cartons, such as the Tetra Pak, provide an alternative packaging option, especially for long-shelf-life milk and milk-based products. They are designed to protect the milk from light, air, and contamination.

Extended Shelf Life: Advances in pasteurization and packaging technologies have enabled the production of milk with an extended shelf life. This includes methods like ultra-high temperature (UHT) processing, which involves heating milk to a high temperature to kill bacteria, allowing it to be stored at room temperature without refrigeration until opened.

Convenience and Portability: The shift to plastic bottles and cartons has increased the convenience and portability of milk. Plastic jugs are easier to handle and transport, making them suitable for both retail and consumer use. Smaller-sized containers, such as single-serving milk bottles, have become popular for on-the-go consumption.

Sustainable Packaging: As environmental concerns grow, there is a focus on developing more sustainable packaging options for milk. Some companies are exploring plant-based plastics, biodegradable materials, and compostable packaging to reduce the environmental impact of milk packaging.

It's worth noting that the specific packaging methods and materials used for bottling milk can vary across regions and brands. Factors such as consumer preferences, local regulations, and infrastructure for recycling and waste management also play a role in shaping the packaging choices within the milk industry.

Bottled Soda, like bottled milk, has undergone changes in packaging and distribution methods over time. Here are some key developments:

Glass Bottles: Historically, soda was primarily sold in glass bottles. Glass bottles were reusable and had a distinctive shape and design. However, the use of glass bottles has declined in many regions due to concerns about breakage, transportation costs, and the environmental impact of production and recycling.

Aluminum Cans: Aluminum cans have become the most common packaging format for soda worldwide. Aluminum cans are lightweight, easily stackable, and provide excellent protection against light and oxygen, which can affect the taste and quality of the soda. They are also highly recyclable, with high recycling rates in many countries.

Plastic Bottles: Plastic bottles, typically made from PET (polyethylene terephthalate), have gained popularity as an alternative to glass bottles. Plastic bottles offer convenience, portability, and shatter resistance. They are widely used for carbonated drinks, including soda. However, plastic bottles have faced criticism due to concerns about their environmental impact, particularly related to plastic waste and recycling challenges.

Different Sizes and Formats: Bottled soda is available in various sizes and formats to cater to different consumer preferences and occasions. These include individual serving sizes (e.g., 12 oz or 355 ml), larger bottles for sharing (e.g., 2 liters), and multipacks of smaller bottles or cans. Some brands also offer soda in specialty packaging, such as slim cans or resealable bottles.

Eco-Friendly Packaging Initiatives: In response to environmental concerns, soda companies have taken steps to improve the sustainability of their packaging. This includes initiatives like using recycled PET in plastic bottles, light-weighting bottles to reduce material usage, and exploring alternative packaging materials, such as plant-based plastics or compostable materials.

Fountain Dispensing: Apart from bottled soda, fountain dispensing has become a popular method for serving soda in restaurants, fast-food chains, and convenience stores. Fountain dispensers mix concentrated syrup with carbonated water, allowing consumers to customize their drink and reduce packaging waste associated with individual bottles or cans.

It's important to note that the specific packaging choices for bottled soda can vary across brands, regions, and markets. Factors such as consumer preferences, cost considerations, local infrastructure for recycling, and sustainability goals influence the packaging decisions made by soda manufacturers.

~ 12 ~

CONTAINERS

Glass containers:

Glass is a versatile material used for packaging various products across industries. Here are some common examples of products that often come in glass containers:

Beverages: Glass bottles are commonly used for packaging a wide range of beverages, including soft drinks, carbonated drinks, juices, spirits, wine, beer, and non-alcoholic beverages. Glass is chosen for these products due to its ability to preserve taste, integrity, and the perception of quality.

Food Products: Many food products are packaged in glass containers for reasons such as preserving freshness, preventing contamination, and enhancing shelf appeal. Examples include sauces, condiments (such as ketchup and mayonnaise), pickles, jams, jellies, honey, baby food, olive oil, vinegar, and various types of preserves.

Cosmetics and Personal Care Products: Glass is a popular choice for packaging cosmetics and personal care items. This includes perfumes, colognes, lotions, serums, oils, skincare products, nail polish, and makeup products. Glass packaging is often preferred for its aesthetic appeal and the ability to protect sensitive formulations.

Pharmaceuticals and Medicines: Many prescription drugs, over-the-counter medications, and supplements are packaged in glass containers. Glass is chemically inert, non-reactive, and provides a reliable barrier against moisture, light, and air. It is used for vials, bottles, ampoules, and other pharmaceutical packaging.

Home Care and Cleaning Products: Glass containers are used for packaging various home care and cleaning products, such as liquid detergents, fabric softeners, surface cleaners, and household chemicals. Glass offers a durable and leak-resistant packaging solution for these products.

Personal Care and Fragrance Products: Glass containers are often utilized for perfumes, colognes, and other fragrance products. Glass allows for the preservation of the fragrance while providing an attractive and luxurious presentation.

Specialty Products: Glass packaging is also used for specialty products, including gourmet food items, artisanal products, high-end alcoholic beverages, premium chocolates, and gourmet spices. Glass containers are often preferred to convey a sense of quality and craftsmanship.

It's important to note that while glass is widely used for packaging these products, alternatives such as plastic, metal, or paper-based packaging may also be utilized depending on the specific product, market demands, and environmental considerations.

Can Containers:

Cans are commonly used for packaging a wide variety of products across different industries. Here are some examples of products that often come in cans:

Beverages: Aluminum or steel cans are frequently used for packaging beverages. This includes carbonated soft drinks, energy drinks, beer, cider, sparkling water, ready-to-drink coffee and tea, canned wine, and various non-alcoholic beverages.

Canned Foods: Canned foods provide a convenient and long-lasting option for preserving and storing various food products. Examples include canned vegetables (corn, peas, beans), fruits (pineapple, peaches, mandarin oranges), soups, sauces (tomato sauce, pasta sauce), meats (tuna, chicken, spam), seafood (sardines, salmon), beans, legumes, and pre-cooked meals.

Canned Pet Food: Pet food, both wet and dry, is often packaged in cans. These cans are specially designed to meet the nutritional needs of pets and provide a longer shelf life for the food.

Preserved Goods: Cans are used for preserving goods like jams, jellies, fruit preserves, fruit fillings, and pie fillings. These products have a longer shelf life and are convenient for storage and consumption.

Aerosol Products: Aerosol cans, typically made of aluminum or steel, are used for packaging a range of products that are dispensed as a spray. This includes personal care products like deodorants, hair sprays, shaving foams, and air fresheners, as well as household items like insecticides, cleaning sprays, and automotive products.

Cooking Ingredients: Certain cooking ingredients are available in cans for easy storage and usage. This includes items like coconut milk, condensed milk, evaporated milk, tomato paste, and cooking oils.

Industrial and Automotive Products: Cans are also used to package various industrial and automotive products, such as paints, varnishes, lubricants, sealants, automotive fluids, and chemicals.

It's important to note that while cans are widely used for packaging these products, there are alternative packaging options available, such as bottles, pouches, and cartons, depending on the specific product and market requirements.

Cardboard Containers:

Cardboard containers, also known as cardboard boxes or cartons, are widely used for packaging, and transporting a variety of products. Cardboard is a versatile material used for packaging a wide variety of products. Here are some examples of products that often come in cardboard packaging:

Food Products: Many food products are packaged in cardboard containers, including cereal boxes, pasta boxes, cake mix boxes, tea and coffee packaging, frozen food boxes, and food delivery boxes.

Beverages: Cardboard packaging is commonly used for beverages such as milk cartons, juice boxes, and Tetra Pak containers for items like fruit juices, dairy alternatives, and soup.

Personal Care and Household Products: Cardboard packaging is prevalent in personal care and household products. Examples include toothpaste boxes, soap and shampoo boxes, tissue boxes, laundry detergent boxes, and cleaning product containers.

Electronics and Appliances: Many electronics and appliances come in cardboard packaging to provide protection during transportation and storage. This includes items like TVs, computers, smartphones, kitchen appliances, and home entertainment systems.

Toys and Games: Cardboard is often used for packaging toys and games. Board games, puzzles, model kits, and children's toys frequently come in cardboard boxes.

Pharmaceuticals and Medicines: Some pharmaceutical products, such as over-the-counter medicines and prescription drugs, are packaged in cardboard boxes. These boxes often contain information about dosage, usage instructions, and warnings.

Clothing and Accessories: Clothing items, shoes, and accessories are often packaged in cardboard boxes. This includes shoeboxes, shirt boxes, jewelry boxes, and hat boxes.

Books and Stationery: Cardboard packaging is commonly used for books, notebooks, notepads, and stationery items. Cardboard boxes are also used for shipping and storing large quantities of books.

Home Decor and Furnishings: Some home decor and furnishings, such as picture frames, lamps, small furniture items, and decorative accessories, are packaged in cardboard boxes for protection during transportation.

Office Supplies: Many office supplies, including pens, markers, file folders, and sticky notes, come in cardboard packaging. Cardboard boxes are also used for storing and organizing office materials.

It's worth noting that while cardboard is a popular packaging material, other materials like plastic, metal, and glass are also used depending on the product and industry. Additionally, companies are increasingly focusing on using sustainable and recyclable packaging materials to reduce environmental impact.

Why can't we put a deposit on all the above and reuse/recycle these containers? It is possible that consumers don't want to be inconvenienced; their behavior is contradictive to a person wanting to do their part to save the planet.

~ 13 ~

PLASTIC VS. PAPER

Back in my youth, stores only used paper bags for groceries. We didn't have plastic bags yet. Later in time there was a concern of global impact by the number of trees that were being cut down to support paper products. This was the introduction to the plastic bags. We have come full circle, and how long before we discover we are cutting down too many trees again?

The switch from paper to plastic has occurred in certain contexts for several reasons. Here are some key factors that have influenced the shift:

Durability and Versatility: Plastic is known for its durability and versatility. It can withstand moisture, is resistant to tearing, and can be molded into various shapes and sizes. These properties make plastic suitable for packaging and applications where durability is required, such as in food packaging or transportation of goods.

Cost-effectiveness: Plastic production and manufacturing processes can be more cost-effective compared to paper. Plastic is lightweight, reducing transportation costs, and it can be produced at scale using efficient manufacturing methods. This cost advantage has contributed to its popularity in many industries.

Performance Characteristics: Plastic can offer specific performance characteristics that paper may not provide. For example, plastic films can provide barrier properties that protect against moisture, air, or light, enhancing the shelf life of certain products. Plastic also offers opportunities for product innovation and customization due to its wide range of properties and capabilities.

Resource Efficiency: In some cases, plastic packaging may require fewer resources to produce compared to paper alternatives. For example, plastic bags can be lighter and require less material compared to paper bags of the same capacity. This reduced material usage can result in lower energy consumption and greenhouse gas emissions during production and transportation.

Hygiene and Food Safety: Plastic packaging is

often preferred for products that require a high level of hygiene and food safety, such as in the medical and food industries. Plastic can provide a protective barrier against contamination, ensuring the integrity and safety of the packaged goods.

However, it is important to note that the increased use of plastic has raised concerns regarding its environmental impact. Plastic waste, especially single-use plastic items, contributes to pollution, litter, and can have harmful effects on ecosystems, wildlife, and human health. The persistent nature of plastics in the environment and their slow decomposition further exacerbate these concerns.

Balancing the advantages of plastic with its environmental impact has led to increasing calls for reducing single-use plastics, improving recycling infrastructure, promoting sustainable alternatives, and encouraging responsible plastic use and disposal practices. It is crucial to find a sustainable balance between the benefits plastic offers and its potential negative consequences for the environment.

Switching back from plastic to paper in certain contexts has gained traction due to growing concerns about plastic pollution and the environmental impact of plastic waste. Here are some reasons why the switch back to paper is being considered:

Biodegradability and Environmental Impact:

Paper is generally biodegradable and can decompose more easily in the environment compared to many plastic materials. By using paper instead of plastic, there is a reduced risk of long-lasting pollution and harm to ecosystems. Paper products, when responsibly sourced and manufactured, can have a lower overall environmental impact.

Renewable and Sustainable Resource: Paper is primarily made from wood fiber derived from trees, which are renewable resources. Responsibly managed forests can provide a sustainable and renewable supply of raw materials for paper production. In contrast, plastic is derived from non-renewable fossil fuels, contributing to carbon emissions and resource depletion.

Recycling Infrastructure: Paper has a well-established and widely accessible recycling infrastructure in many regions. Recycling paper products can help reduce the demand for virgin fibers, conserve resources, and decrease energy consumption compared to producing paper from virgin materials. The recycling process for paper can also have lower environmental impacts compared to plastic recycling.

Perception and Consumer Preference: Some consumers prefer paper packaging and products due to their perceived environmental benefits. Businesses and brands may switch to paper-based alternatives to align with consumer preferences and environmental values, enhancing their brand image and customer loyalty.

Regulatory Measures and Bans: Governments and regulatory bodies have implemented or proposed measures to restrict or ban certain single-use plastic items. This has prompted businesses to seek alternative materials, including paper, to comply with regulations and demonstrate their commitment to sustainability.

Innovation in Paper Products: Advancements in paper technology have expanded the range of applications for paper-based materials. Innovative paper products, such as compostable or bio-based coatings, water-resistant paper, and eco-friendly packaging solutions, are being developed to offer alternatives to plastic while maintaining performance and functionality.

It's important to note that the switch from plastic to paper should be approached in a thoughtful and holistic manner. Life cycle assessments, considering factors such as resource consumption, energy use, and greenhouse gas emissions, should be conducted to ensure that the shift to paper-based alternatives is indeed environmentally beneficial. Additionally, it is crucial to address other sustainability considerations, such as responsible sourcing, forest management practices, and the potential impacts on water usage and air pollution associated with paper production.

The debate between paper and plastic is centered around their environmental impact, specifically regarding their production, use, and disposal. Here are some key points to consider:

Production: Both paper and plastic have environmental consequences during their production. Paper production requires cutting down trees, which can lead to deforestation and habitat loss. On the other hand, plastic is made from petroleum products, a non-renewable resource that contributes to greenhouse gas emissions during extraction and processing.

Energy and Water Usage: Paper production generally requires more energy and water compared to plastic. The pulp and paper industry are water-intensive, consuming large amounts of water for processing and recycling. Plastic production involves energy-intensive processes like refining crude oil and manufacturing polymers.

Durability and Reusability: Plastic is known for its durability and can withstand multiple uses, making it suitable for products like reusable bags and containers. However, plastic waste can persist in the environment for hundreds of years, leading to pollution and harm to wildlife. Paper, while less durable, is biodegradable and can be recycled more easily.

Recycling: Both paper and plastic can be recycled, but the processes and effectiveness vary. Paper recycling generally has a higher recycling rate compared to plastic. Recycled paper can be turned into new paper products multiple times, reducing the need for fresh raw materials. Plastic recycling is more challenging due to different types and grades of plastics, limited recycling infrastructure, and contamination issues.

Waste Management: Improper disposal of both paper and plastic contributes to environmental problems. Plastic waste, especially single-use items like bags and packaging, can end up in landfills, oceans, or natural habitats, posing a threat to marine life and ecosystems. Paper waste in landfills can release methane, a potent greenhouse gas.

Alternative Solutions: There are ongoing efforts to reduce reliance on both paper and plastic. For paper, sustainable forestry practices, recycling programs, and using alternative fibers (such as agricultural waste or bamboo) can help mitigate environmental impact. Plastic alternatives include biodegradable plastics, compostable materials, and promoting reusable options like cloth bags.

There are several alternative solutions to the use of

paper and plastic that can help reduce environmental impacts. Here are some examples:

Biodegradable or Compostable Materials: Biodegradable materials, such as certain types of bioplastics, can break down naturally in the environment over time. Compostable materials, designed to decompose in specific composting conditions, offer another environmentally friendly option. These materials can be used for packaging, utensils, and other single-use items.

Plant-based and Renewable Materials: Utilizing plant-based materials, such as bamboo, sugarcane bagasse, or hemp, offers renewable and sustainable alternatives. These materials can be used for various applications, including packaging, paper products, and even as substitutes for plastic in some cases.

Reusable Containers and Packaging: Encouraging the use of reusable containers and packaging can significantly reduce waste. This can involve promoting refillable water bottles, reusable shopping bags, and encouraging customers to bring their own containers for bulk purchases.

Innovative Materials and Technologies: Ongoing research and development are focused on creating new materials and technologies that are environmentally friendly. This includes exploring options like edible packaging, algae-based materials, and mycelium (mushroom-based) packaging, which have the potential to offer sustainable alternatives to traditional paper and plastic.

Digital Solutions: Embracing digital alternatives can help reduce paper consumption. Digital documents, e-tickets, e-books, and online transactions can minimize the need for paper-based materials.

Packaging Reduction: Innovative packaging design and materials can help minimize the need for excessive packaging or utilize more eco-friendly options. Lightweighting packaging, optimizing design to reduce material use, and employing biodegradable or compostable packaging materials are effective strategies.

Consumer Education and Behavior Change: Educating consumers about the environmental impact of paper and plastic and promoting sustainable choices can drive behavior change. Encouraging recycling, promoting responsible consumption, and raising awareness about reusable alternatives can help reduce reliance on single-use items.

It is important to consider the life cycle impacts of alternative materials, including their sourcing, production, use, and disposal, to ensure they offer sustainable solutions. A comprehensive and holistic approach, considering multiple factors such as resource consumption, energy use, emissions, and waste management, is necessary for evaluating and implementing effective alternatives to paper and plastic.

Support and choose products from companies that prioritize sustainable practices, engage in responsible sourcing, promote recycling, and actively work towards minimizing their environmental footprint. Additionally, individuals can contribute by reducing paper consumption, recycling paper products, and advocating for sustainable forestry practices.

The environmental impact of paper versus plastic varies depending on various factors, such as the specific product, local waste management systems, recycling infrastructure, and individual behavior. A comprehensive approach would involve reducing consumption, promoting recycling, supporting sustainable alternatives, and advocating for improved waste management practices.

~ 14 ~

THE PLASTIC ISLAND

Have you ever heard of the Plastic Island? The term "Plastic Island" is often used to refer to the Great Pacific Garbage Patch, which is a vast accumulation of floating plastic debris in the Pacific Ocean. Here are some key points about the Great Pacific Garbage Patch:

Definition and Size: The Great Pacific Garbage Patch is not a solid island of plastic but rather a large area of marine debris concentrated by ocean currents. It is in the North Pacific Ocean between California and Hawaii. The exact size is difficult to determine due to the scattered and constantly moving nature of the debris, but it is estimated to cover a significant area, potentially spanning millions of square kilometers.

Composition: The garbage patch consists of various types of plastic, including bottles, bags, packaging materials, fishing nets, and microplastics. These plastics can take hundreds of years to break down, persisting in the environment and causing harm to marine life.

Formation: The garbage patch is formed because of ocean currents, particularly the North Pacific Gyre, which traps and accumulates floating debris. Winds and currents converge in this region, causing the debris to accumulate over time.

Environmental Impact: The presence of plastic debris in the Great Pacific Garbage Patch has detrimental effects on marine ecosystems. Marine animals can become entangled in or ingest plastic, leading to injury, suffocation, or starvation. Additionally, plastics can release toxic chemicals into the water, affecting marine life at various levels of the food chain.

Global Issue: Plastic pollution in the oceans is not limited to the Great Pacific Garbage Patch. Similar accumulations of plastic debris have been observed in other oceanic regions as well. Plastic waste can travel long distances, carried by currents, and impact coastal areas and remote islands worldwide.

Cleanup Efforts: Various organizations and initiatives are working towards reducing plastic pollution and cleaning up the oceans. These efforts include developing technologies to remove plastic debris, promoting waste management and recycling practices, and advocating for policies to reduce plastic consumption and promote sustainable alternatives.

It's important to note that the Great Pacific Garbage Patch represents just one aspect of the larger issue of plastic pollution in the oceans. Addressing plastic waste requires a multi-faceted approach that involves individuals, businesses, governments, and international cooperation. Efforts should focus on reducing plastic consumption, improving waste management systems, promoting recycling and circular economy models, and investing in research and innovation to find sustainable alternatives to plastic.

~ 15 ~

WAYS TO RECYCLE

There are several ways individuals can actively participate in recycling efforts. Here are some common ways to recycle:

Curbside Recycling: Many communities offer curbside recycling programs where residents can place recyclable materials in designated bins or containers. Check with your local waste management or recycling agency to find out what materials are accepted and how they should be prepared for collection.

Recycling Drop-Off Centers: Recycling drop-off centers are locations where you can bring your recyclables for proper disposal. These centers typically have separate bins or containers for different types of materials, such as paper, plastic, glass, and metal. Find the nearest drop-off center in your area and familiarize yourself with the accepted materials.

Recycling at Work or School: Encourage recycling at your workplace or school by setting up designated recycling bins for paper, plastic, and other recyclable materials. Educate your colleagues or classmates about the importance of recycling and provide clear guidelines on what can and cannot be recycled.

Composting: Composting is a form of recycling that involves converting organic waste, such as food scraps and yard trimmings, into nutrient-rich compost. Composting reduces waste sent to landfills and produces valuable soil amendment for gardening and landscaping. Consider starting a compost pile or using a composting bin to manage organic waste at home.

Electronics Recycling: Electronics contain valuable and potentially hazardous materials that should be recycled properly. Many communities have designated electronic waste recycling programs or collection events where you can dispose of old computers, phones, batteries, and other electronic devices. Check with local electronic recycling facilities or retailers that accept electronic waste.

Clothing and Textile Recycling: Instead of throwing away old clothes and textiles, consider donating them to thrift stores, charities, or textile recycling centers. These organizations may repurpose or recycle the items, reducing textile waste and supporting those in need.

Buy Recycled Products: Support recycling efforts by purchasing products made from recycled materials. Look for products with recycled content labels or packaging made from recycled materials. By creating demand for recycled products, you contribute to closing the recycling loop and promoting a circular economy.

Remember, it's important to familiarize yourself with the specific recycling guidelines in your area. Different regions may have different rules and regulations regarding acceptable materials and recycling methods. By actively participating in recycling and encouraging others to do the same, you can contribute to the conservation of resources, reduction of waste, and the overall well-being of the environment.

CHALLENGES OF RECYCLING

While recycling plays an essential role in waste management and resource conservation, it does face several significant challenges and problems. Here are some of the major issues associated with recycling:

Contamination: Contamination of recyclable materials is a widespread problem. When non-recyclable items or materials that are not properly sorted are mixed with recyclables, it reduces the quality and value of the recycled materials. Contamination can occur due to improper sorting at the source, inadequate recycling education, or limited recycling infrastructure.

Lack of Universal Standards: Recycling practices and regulations vary across different regions and even within different municipalities. The lack of consistent and standardized recycling guidelines can lead to confusion among consumers and result in improper disposal or ineffective recycling efforts.

Limited Infrastructure: Insufficient recycling infrastructure, such as collection systems, sorting facilities, and recycling plants, can hinder recycling efforts. In some areas, there may be a lack of convenient recycling options or inadequate capacity to process recyclable materials, leading to lower recycling rates.

Economic Viability: The economic viability of recycling can be a challenge. Recycling processes often require significant investments in collection, sorting, transportation, and processing, and the revenue generated from selling recycled materials may not always cover the costs. Fluctuating commodity prices for recycled materials can also impact the economic feasibility of recycling programs.

Single-Use Plastics: Single-use plastics, such as disposable packaging and plastic bags, pose a particular challenge for recycling. These items are often made of complex materials that are difficult to recycle or are not accepted by recycling facilities. Their widespread use contributes to the accumulation of plastic waste and limits recycling options.

Lack of Market Demand: The demand for recycled materials can fluctuate, affecting the market for recyclables. If there is a limited demand for certain types of recycled materials, it can become challenging to find buyers and create a sustainable market for those materials.

Limited Education and Awareness: Many people are still not fully aware of the importance of recycling or may not understand proper recycling practices. Insufficient education and awareness campaigns can result in low recycling participation rates and increased contamination of recycling streams.

To address these challenges and improve recycling, various actions can be taken, including:

Implementing comprehensive recycling education and awareness programs to promote proper recycling practices and reduce contamination.

Investing in recycling infrastructure and expanding collection and processing capabilities to accommodate a wider range of materials.

Encouraging product design that prioritizes recyclability and the use of recycled materials.

Developing and enforcing consistent recycling regulations and standards to improve efficiency and effectiveness.

Promoting the use of recycled materials through

government procurement policies and incentives for businesses to create demand for recycled products.

Supporting research and innovation in recycling technologies to improve efficiency and the quality of recycled materials.

By addressing these challenges and adopting a holistic approach to recycling, it is possible to enhance recycling rates, reduce waste, conserve resources, and mitigate environmental impacts.

But there is a cost to recycling. The cost of recycling can vary depending on various factors such as location, infrastructure, materials being recycled, and the specific recycling processes involved. Here are some key cost considerations related to recycling:

Collection and Sorting: The collection and sorting of recyclable materials can incur costs. This includes the operation and maintenance of recycling trucks, personnel wages, fuel, and equipment. The more extensive the recycling program and the larger the area covered, the higher the associated costs.

Processing and Transportation: Once collected, recyclable materials need to be processed, which can involve further sorting, cleaning, and processing to transform them into reusable materials. Processing costs can vary depending on the type of material and the level of contamination. Transportation costs are also incurred when transporting recyclables to processing facilities.

Market Value of Recyclables: The market value of recyclable materials is an important factor in determining the overall cost of recycling. The prices of recycled materials are influenced by factors such as global demand, commodity prices, and the quality of the materials. Fluctuations in market prices can impact the financial viability of recycling programs.

Infrastructure Investments: Establishing and maintaining recycling infrastructure, such as recycling plants, sorting facilities, and recycling equipment, requires significant investments. These initial capital costs, as well as ongoing operational expenses, contribute to the overall cost of recycling.

Contamination and Waste Management: Contamination of recyclable materials with non-recyclables can increase the cost of recycling. Contaminated materials often require additional sorting or may be rejected for recycling, leading to increased processing costs or the need for landfill disposal. Effective education and outreach programs can help minimize contamination and associated costs.

Subsidies and Incentives: Governments or waste management authorities may provide subsidies, grants, or incentives to support recycling efforts. These financial incentives can help offset some of the costs associated with recycling and encourage greater participation.

It's important to note that while recycling can involve costs, it also provides economic benefits and environmental advantages. Recycling conserves natural resources, reduces waste sent to landfills, and promotes the development of a circular economy. The overall cost-effectiveness of recycling depends on factors such as economies of scale, efficient operations, market conditions, and public engagement.

To optimize recycling programs and minimize costs, it is crucial to invest in efficient infrastructure, educate the public about proper recycling practices, improve sorting and processing technologies, and foster partnerships between government, industry, and the community. By doing so, the costs of recycling can be managed effectively while realizing the long-term benefits of a sustainable waste management system. What do you do as an individual?

Doing your part in recycling is an important step towards sustainable waste management and environmental conservation. Here are some actions you can take to contribute to recycling efforts:

Know the Guidelines: Familiarize yourself with the

recycling guidelines in your area. Understand what materials are accepted for recycling, how they should be sorted, and any specific requirements or restrictions. Check with your local waste management or recycling agency for detailed information.

Properly Sort and Prepare Recyclables: Ensure that you sort and prepare recyclables correctly. Separate materials such as paper, plastic, glass, and metal into designated recycling bins or containers. Remove any contaminants, such as food residue or non-recyclable parts, to minimize contamination.

Reduce, Reuse, and Repurpose: Remember that recycling is just one part of the waste management hierarchy. Before recycling, focus on reducing your consumption, reusing items whenever possible, and finding creative ways to repurpose or upcycle materials. By minimizing waste generation, you reduce the need for recycling in the first place.

Recycle at Home: Set up recycling bins in your home to collect recyclable materials. Educate your family members about proper recycling practices and encourage their participation. Make recycling a routine part of your household activities.

Support Local Recycling Programs: Participate in curbside recycling programs or utilize local recycling drop-off centers. Be aware of any special recycling events or initiatives in your community, such as electronic waste or hazardous waste collection days. Take advantage of these opportunities to dispose of specific materials responsibly.

Reduce Contamination: Contamination can compromise the recycling process and reduce the quality of recycled materials. Make sure to follow the guidelines for accepted materials and avoid placing non-recyclables or hazardous items in recycling bins. Properly rinse out containers, remove caps and lids, and flatten cardboard boxes to maximize space and minimize contamination.

Purchase Recycled Products: Support the demand for recycled materials by actively seeking out products made from recycled content. Look for products with recycling symbols or labels indicating that they are made from recycled materials. By choosing recycled products, you create a market for recycled materials and encourage the recycling industry.

Educate and Spread Awareness: Share your knowledge about recycling with others. Educate friends, family, and colleagues about the importance of recycling and proper recycling practices. Encourage them to join you in recycling efforts and help create a culture of recycling in your community.

Remember that individual actions, when combined, can make a significant impact. By doing your part in recycling and inspiring others to do the same, you contribute to a more sustainable and environmentally conscious society.

~ 17 ~

LANDFILLS

Landfills have a significant impact on the environment and can contribute to various environmental issues. While they are necessary for waste management in many parts of the world, the management and operation of landfills play a crucial role in minimizing their negative effects. Here are some ways in which landfills can impact the environment:

Air and Water Pollution: Landfills produce methane gas, a potent greenhouse gas that contributes to climate change. They also emit other air pollutants, such as volatile organic compounds (VOCs) and hazardous air pollutants (HAPs).

Soil Contamination: Improperly managed landfills can result in soil contamination. Hazardous substances from the waste can seep into the soil, affecting its quality and potentially impacting plant and animal life in the surrounding area. This contamination can persist for long periods and require costly remediation efforts.

Habitat Destruction: The construction and expansion of landfills often require clearing large areas of land, which can lead to habitat destruction and loss of biodiversity. Landfills can disrupt natural ecosystems, displace wildlife, and reduce the availability of suitable habitats for plants and animals.

Visual and Aesthetic Impact: Landfills can have a negative visual impact on the surrounding landscape, affecting the aesthetic value of the area. This can impact tourism, property values, and the overall quality of life for nearby communities.

Resource depletion: Landfills represent the inefficient use of resources since they bury materials that could potentially be recycled, reused, or repurposed. The disposal of valuable resources in landfills contributes to the depletion of natural resources and exacerbates the need for raw material extraction.

Leachate management: Landfills produce leachate, a liquid that forms as waste decomposes and meets precipitation or other liquids. Proper management of leachate is crucial to prevent its escape into the environment and to avoid contamination of nearby water bodies.

To mitigate the environmental impact of landfills, various measures and alternative waste management approaches are being implemented:

Waste Reduction and Recycling: Encouraging waste reduction and promoting recycling initiatives can divert a significant portion of waste from landfills. By reducing the amount of waste generated and recycling materials, the need for landfill space can be minimized.

Waste-to-Energy Conversion: Some landfills incorporate waste-to-energy technologies, such as waste incineration with energy recovery. These processes convert waste into energy while reducing the volume of waste that needs to be landfilled.

Improved Landfill Design and Operation: Implementing advanced landfill designs, such as lining systems and gas collection systems, can help reduce the release of pollutants into the environment. Proper management practices, including leachate and gas control measures, can minimize environmental impacts.

Landfill Gas Management: Landfills can capture and utilize methane gas generated from waste decomposition as a renewable energy source, mitigating its impact on climate change.

Landfill Remediation and Closure: Decommissioning and rehabilitating old landfills require proper closure procedures, including soil capping, groundwater monitoring, and site remediation to restore the area's environmental quality.

Education: Encouraging public education and awareness about waste management and the importance of reducing, reusing, and recycling.

Transition to Sustainable Waste Management: Governments and communities are exploring sustainable waste management practices, such as waste separation, composting, and the development of circular economy models to reduce reliance on landfills.

While landfills are currently a necessary part of waste management, their environmental impact can be reduced through improved waste management practices, resource conservation, and a transition to more sustainable approaches. It's important for governments, communities, and individuals to prioritize waste reduction, recycling, and the development of innovative waste management strategies to minimize the negative effects of landfills on our planet.

Converting landfills into usable spaces or repurposing them for alternative purposes can be a challenging but rewarding endeavor. While there are various approaches to landfill conversion, here are a few potential options:

Landfill Gas Utilization: Many landfills produce

methane gas as organic waste decomposes. Instead of allowing the methane to escape into the atmosphere, it can be captured and used as a source of renewable energy. Landfill gas can be collected, treated, and utilized for electricity generation or as a fuel for heating and other industrial processes.

Renewable Energy Projects: Landfill sites can be suitable for hosting renewable energy projects, such as solar or wind farms. These projects can make use of the available land without disturbing the landfill itself, helping to generate clean energy and contribute to sustainability goals.

Parks and Recreational Spaces: Once a landfill has undergone proper closure and remediation, it may be transformed into public parks, green spaces, or recreational areas. Landfills can be landscaped and rehabilitated to create walking trails, sports fields, picnic areas, or nature preserves. These spaces can provide opportunities for community engagement, leisure activities, and environmental education.

Solar Panel Installations: Landfill sites can be suitable for installing solar panels due to their typically large areas of open land. Solar arrays can be set up on top of capped landfills, taking advantage of the space while generating clean energy.

Commercial and Residential Developments: In some

cases, landfills may be converted into commercial or residential developments after proper remediation and regulatory approvals. This typically involves significant engineering and remediation efforts to ensure the safety and stability of the site for construction and habitation.

It's important to note that the conversion of landfills requires thorough planning, engineering assessments, and compliance with local regulations and environmental standards. Each site is unique, and the feasibility of conversion depends on factors such as the landfill's location, size, environmental impact, and potential reuse options.

Successful landfill conversion projects often involve collaboration between government agencies, environmental experts, developers, and the local community. Prioritizing environmental sustainability, safety, and long-term viability are key considerations when repurposing landfills to minimize any potential risks and maximize the positive impact on the surrounding area.

Converting a landfill to usable real-estate can go horribly wrong, just ask the families of Love Canal. Love Canal is a neighborhood in Niagara Falls, New York, that gained notoriety in the 1970s due to a major environmental disaster. It was the site of a hazardous waste landfill that caused significant health and environmental impacts on the community. Here are some key points about the Love Canal incident:

History: Love Canal was originally intended to be a planned community in the 1950s. However, it was never fully developed, and in the 1940s and 1950s, Hooker Chemical Company used the abandoned canal as a disposal site for chemical waste.

Toxic Waste Contamination: The chemicals buried at Love Canal included hazardous substances such as dioxins, pesticides, and various industrial chemicals. The waste was inadequately contained and led to contamination of the soil, groundwater, and nearby sewers.

Health Impacts: Residents of Love Canal began experiencing a range of health issues, including birth defects, miscarriages, respiratory problems, and various other ailments. Children in the area showed higher rates of birth defects and developmental disabilities.

Environmental Impact: The toxic waste at Love Canal posed significant risks to the surrounding environment. Chemicals from the landfill contaminated the groundwater, which, in turn, led to the contamination of nearby creeks and the Niagara River.

Activism and Relocation: Concerned residents formed the Love Canal Homeowners Association and fought for their voices to be heard. Eventually, the U.S. government declared a state of emergency in 1978, leading to the evacuation and relocation of over 800 families from the affected area.

Legal and Regulatory Changes: The Love Canal incident led to significant changes in environmental legislation and regulations. It played a pivotal role in the creation of the Comprehensive Environmental Response, Compensation, and Liability Act (CERCLA), commonly known as Superfund, which provides funds for the cleanup of hazardous waste sites.

Environmental Legacy: The Love Canal incident serves as a reminder of the potential long-term consequences of improper waste disposal practices and the importance of proper environmental management. It raised awareness about the need for stricter regulations and improved waste management practices to protect public health and the environment.

The Love Canal incident had a profound impact on environmental policy, public health awareness, and the perception of hazardous waste disposal. It highlighted the importance of proper waste management, community engagement, and government accountability in safeguarding public health and the environment. I know growing up in Niagara Falls, you knew someone that knew someone that lived in Love Canal.

~ 18 ~

NOT SO EASY

There are certain items that can be challenging to recycle due to various reasons. Here are some examples of things that are generally considered hard to recycle:

Plastic bags and film: Plastic bags and thin plastic film, such as food wrappers and cling wraps, are problematic for recycling facilities. They can get tangled in the sorting machinery, leading to breakdowns and inefficiencies. Many grocery stores provide collection bins specifically for plastic bags and film.

Styrofoam (Expanded Polystyrene): Styrofoam is difficult to recycle because it is lightweight and bulky, making it cost-prohibitive to transport and process. Some recycling centers accept certain forms of clean and uncontaminated Styrofoam, but it is not widely recyclable.

Disposable coffee cups: Disposable coffee cups are often lined with a plastic coating that makes them waterproof but difficult to recycle. The combination of paper and plastic materials makes it challenging for recycling facilities to separate and process them effectively.

Tetra Pak cartons: Tetra Pak cartons, commonly used for milk, juice, and other beverages, are made of multiple layers of paper, plastic, and aluminum. The complex composition makes it difficult to separate the materials during the recycling process, limiting their recyclability in some areas.

Broken glass: While glass is recyclable, broken glass can be problematic. Small glass shards can mix with other recyclables and pose a safety hazard to workers in recycling facilities. It is generally recommended to dispose of broken glass separately, ensuring proper containment and labeling.

Electronic waste (e-waste): Electronics contain various components and hazardous materials that require specialized recycling processes. While e-waste recycling programs exist, they may not be easily accessible to everyone, and improper disposal can lead to environmental pollution.

Clothing and textiles: While clothing and textiles can be recycled, the infrastructure for textile recycling is not as widespread as other materials. Many garments end up in landfills, where they contribute to waste accumulation and environmental issues.

Composite materials: Items made of multiple materials that are difficult to separate, such as laminated plastics or metal-plastic hybrids, pose challenges for recycling. The different materials may require complex and energy-intensive processes to extract and recycle individually.

It is important to note that recycling capabilities can vary by location. Some items considered hard to recycle in one area may have recycling options available elsewhere. Always check with your local recycling guidelines and facilities to determine the accepted items in your specific area, otherwise it just ends up in a landfill somewhere.

~ 19 ~

PROTECTING THE ECOSYSTEM

Protecting the ecosystem is a topic that elicits various arguments and perspectives. Here are some common arguments related to the importance of ecosystem protection:

Biodiversity and Ecological Balance: Supporters of ecosystem protection emphasize the intrinsic value of biodiversity and the need to maintain healthy and balanced ecosystems. They argue that preserving diverse species and their habitats is essential for the stability and resilience of ecosystems, as well as for the overall health of the planet.

Ecosystem Services: Ecosystems provide vital services that support human well-being and economic prosperity. Advocates argue that protecting ecosystems ensures the provision of services such as clean air and water, climate regulation, soil fertility, pollination, and natural pest control. They assert that maintaining these services is crucial for human survival and sustainable development.

Climate Change Mitigation and Adaptation: Ecosystems play a significant role in mitigating climate change by absorbing and storing carbon dioxide. Supporters argue that protecting forests, wetlands, and other natural habitats can help sequester carbon and reduce greenhouse gas emissions. Additionally, intact ecosystems can provide natural buffers against the impacts of climate change, such as floods, storms, and droughts.

Conservation of Endangered Species: Protecting ecosystems involves safeguarding endangered species and their habitats. Advocates argue that preserving biodiversity is vital for maintaining ecological balance, preventing species extinctions, and preserving genetic diversity that can be crucial for future scientific and medical advancements.

Sustainable Resource Management: Ecosystem protection is often linked to sustainable resource management. Supporters argue that responsible management of natural resources, such as fisheries, forests, and water sources, ensures their long-term availability and prevents overexploitation or depletion. They highlight the importance of balancing human needs with the conservation of ecosystems.

Ethical and Aesthetic Values: Arguments for ecosystem protection often include ethical considerations, recognizing the intrinsic value of nature and the moral obligation to protect it for future generations. Supporters also emphasize the aesthetic and recreational values of natural landscapes and the role they play in providing inspiration, solace, and cultural heritage.

Economic Benefits: Some argue that ecosystem protection can bring economic benefits. They emphasize the value of nature-based tourism, sustainable agriculture, and ecosystem-based businesses. Additionally, they argue that investing in ecosystem restoration and conservation can create jobs, support local economies, and enhance the resilience of communities.

It's important to note that arguments surrounding ecosystem protection may also involve discussions on land use, development pressures, indigenous rights, policy frameworks, and the balance between conservation and human needs. Engaging in constructive dialogue and considering multiple perspectives is essential for finding effective solutions that promote both environmental sustainability and human well-being.

An ecosystem is a complex and interconnected community of living organisms (plants, animals, microorganisms) and their physical environment (air, water, soil, climate) in which they interact and exchange energy and nutrients. It encompasses both the biotic (living) and abiotic (non-living) components of a particular geographic area or habitat.

Key components of an ecosystem include:

Organisms: Ecosystems are composed of a variety of organisms that interact with each other and their environment. This includes producers (such as plants and algae) that convert sunlight into energy through photosynthesis, consumers (such as herbivores, carnivores, and omnivores) that feed on other organisms, and decomposers (such as bacteria and fungi) that break down organic matter.

Habitat: An ecosystem has a specific physical location or habitat where organisms live. This includes terrestrial ecosystems like forests, grasslands, and deserts, as well as aquatic ecosystems like lakes, rivers, oceans, and wetlands. Each habitat has unique conditions, resources, and adaptations that shape the organisms present in it.

Energy Flow: Ecosystems rely on the flow of energy through the food chain or food web. Energy enters the ecosystem through the primary producers, who convert sunlight into chemical energy through photosynthesis. This energy is transferred from one organism to another as they are consumed by predators or decomposers, creating a network of energy flow.

Nutrient Cycling: Ecosystems involve the cycling and recycling of nutrients. Elements such as carbon, nitrogen, phosphorus, and others are taken up by organisms, utilized in their biological processes, and eventually returned to the environment through decomposition and other processes. This nutrient cycling is essential for maintaining the balance and productivity of the ecosystem.

Interactions and Relationships: Organisms within an ecosystem interact with each other in various ways. This includes predation, competition for resources, mutualism (mutually beneficial relationships), parasitism, and more. These interactions shape the dynamics of the ecosystem, influencing population sizes, species diversity, and community structure.

Environmental Factors: The abiotic factors in an ecosystem, such as temperature, rainfall, sunlight, soil composition, and topography, play a crucial role in shaping the characteristics and distribution of organisms. These environmental factors determine the conditions under which organisms can survive, reproduce, and thrive.

Ecosystems can vary greatly in size, from small microhabitats like a tree canopy to vast biomes like a tropical rainforest or a coral reef. They can be highly diverse and resilient, providing essential services such as water purification, carbon sequestration, nutrient cycling, and habitat for biodiversity.

Understanding ecosystems and their functioning is essential for managing and conserving natural resources, protecting biodiversity, and promoting sustainable development.

Buy protecting the ecosystem, the ecosystem protests us. Ecosystems provide protection to various components within them, including:

Species and Biodiversity: Ecosystems serve as habitats and provide essential resources and conditions for the survival and reproduction of a wide range of plant and animal species. Different ecosystems support diverse communities of organisms, allowing them to thrive and maintain healthy populations. Ecosystems protect species by offering shelter, food sources, and suitable environmental conditions.

Natural Resources: Ecosystems protect and sustainably manage natural resources that are vital for human well-being, such as freshwater, fertile soils, forests, and fisheries. These resources are essential for food production, clean water supply, climate regulation, and other societal needs. Healthy ecosystems play a critical role in ensuring the availability and sustainable use of these resources.

Climate and Weather Regulation: Ecosystems contribute to climate regulation by absorbing and storing carbon dioxide, a greenhouse gas that contributes to climate change. Forests, wetlands, and oceans act as carbon sinks, helping to mitigate the impacts of climate change. Additionally, ecosystems influence local weather patterns, temperature regulation, and precipitation distribution, providing protection against extreme weather events.

Water Resources and Watershed Protection: Ecosystems play a vital role in maintaining water quality and regulating the quantity and flow of water within watersheds. Forests and wetlands, for example, act as natural filters, purifying water and reducing sediment and nutrient runoff into streams and rivers. They also help regulate water cycles, prevent soil erosion, and mitigate the risks of flooding and droughts.

Soil Conservation: Ecosystems, particularly forests and grasslands, protect soil from erosion by wind and water. The vegetation cover and root systems of plants help stabilize soil, preventing the loss of topsoil and maintaining soil fertility. Healthy soils are essential for agriculture, supporting food production and sustaining ecosystems.

Coastal Protection: Coastal ecosystems, such as mangroves, coral reefs, and salt marshes, provide natural barriers and protect coastlines from erosion, storm surges, and tidal waves. These ecosystems act as buffers, reducing the impacts of coastal hazards and providing critical protection for human communities and infrastructure.

Human Health: Ecosystems contribute to human health by providing clean air, clean water, and natural spaces for recreation and relaxation. Access to nature and green spaces has been linked to various physical and mental health benefits, including stress reduction, improved cognitive function, and enhanced well-being.

Overall, ecosystems protect and sustain the interconnected web of life, providing essential services and benefits to both nature and humans. Conserving and protecting ecosystems is crucial for maintaining a balanced and sustainable planet. Here are some keyways to protect ecosystems:

Conservation of protected areas: Establishing and effectively managing protected areas, such as national parks, wildlife reserves, and marine sanctuaries, helps safeguard critical habitats and species. These areas provide refuge for wildlife, support biodiversity, and allow ecosystems to thrive.

Sustainable land use and habitat conservation: Promote sustainable land use practices that minimize habitat destruction, such as deforestation, urban sprawl, and conversion of natural areas into agricultural or industrial lands. Protecting and restoring habitats, including forests, wetlands, coral reefs, and grasslands, is essential for maintaining ecosystem health.

Biodiversity conservation: Protecting and conserving biodiversity is crucial for ecosystem stability. Efforts should focus on preserving endangered species, preventing the spread of invasive species, and restoring degraded habitats to support diverse ecosystems.

Sustainable agriculture and forestry: Encourage sustainable agricultural practices that minimize the use of harmful pesticides and fertilizers, promote crop rotation, and preserve soil health. Similarly, sustainable forestry practices, including selective logging and reforestation, can help maintain forest ecosystems and prevent deforestation.

Responsible fishing and marine conservation: Implement and enforce fishing regulations that promote sustainable fishing practices, protect vulnerable species, and prevent overfishing. Establish marine protected areas to conserve marine biodiversity, prevent habitat degradation, and restore degraded coastal ecosystems.

Pollution prevention and control: Minimize pollution of air, water, and soil to protect ecosystems from contamination. Implement and enforce regulations on industrial emissions, waste management, and the use of harmful chemicals to reduce pollution impacts on ecosystems.

Climate change mitigation and adaptation: Addressing climate change is essential for ecosystem protection. Mitigation efforts should focus on reducing greenhouse gas emissions through renewable energy adoption, energy efficiency, and sustainable transportation. Adaptation measures, such as protecting coastal areas from sea-level rise and supporting the resilience of ecosystems, are also crucial.

Education and awareness: Promote environmental education and awareness to foster a sense of responsibility and stewardship towards ecosystems. Encourage sustainable behaviors, such as reducing waste, conserving resources, and supporting eco-friendly practices.

Collaboration and partnerships: Foster collaboration between governments, conservation organizations, local communities, and stakeholders to develop and implement effective ecosystem protection strategies. Engage in partnerships that promote sustainable practices, research, and conservation initiatives.

By implementing these measures and encouraging sustainable practices at individual, community, and societal levels, we can contribute to the protection and preservation of ecosystems, ensuring a healthier and more sustainable planet for future generations.

It's not that easy. Protecting the ecosystem is a complex and challenging task that requires addressing various interconnected issues. Some key challenges associated with ecosystem protection include:

Habitat destruction and fragmentation: Human activities such as deforestation, urbanization, and infrastructure development lead to the destruction and fragmentation of natural habitats. This disrupts ecosystems, displaces species, and reduces biodiversity.

Pollution and contamination: Pollution from industries, agriculture, and improper waste management can severely impact ecosystems. Water pollution, air pollution, and soil contamination harm aquatic life, terrestrial ecosystems, and have long-term ecological consequences.

Invasive species: The introduction of non-native species can have detrimental effects on ecosystems. Invasive species can outcompete native species for resources, disrupt natural food chains, and alter ecosystem dynamics.

Climate change: Global warming and climate change pose significant challenges to ecosystem protection.

Rising temperatures, altered precipitation patterns, and extreme weather events can disrupt habitats, change species distributions, and contribute to the loss of biodiversity.

Overexploitation of natural resources: Unsustainable extraction of natural resources, such as overfishing, illegal logging, and excessive mining, can deplete ecosystems and threaten the survival of species dependent on these resources.

Lack of awareness and education: Limited public awareness and understanding of the importance of ecosystems can hinder conservation efforts. Education and awareness programs are crucial to foster a sense of environmental responsibility and promote sustainable practices.

Insufficient funding and resources: Adequate financial resources, staffing, and infrastructure are necessary for effective ecosystem protection. Limited funding can hamper conservation initiatives, including protected area management, research, and enforcement of environmental regulations.

Conflicts between conservation and development: Balancing conservation efforts with economic development can be challenging. In some cases, there may be conflicts of interest between conserving ecosystems and pursuing activities like infrastructure projects, agriculture expansion, or resource extraction.

Global coordination and governance: Many ecological challenges transcend national boundaries, requiring international cooperation and governance mechanisms. Ensuring effective coordination, information sharing, and policy alignment among countries is essential for addressing global environmental issues.

Addressing these challenges requires a multifaceted approach involving collaboration between governments, communities, NGOs, and other stakeholders. It involves implementing and enforcing environmental regulations, promoting sustainable practices, investing in research and conservation efforts, and fostering public engagement and participation in ecosystem protection.

~ 20 ~

AGRICULTURE AND FOOD

Agriculture and food production are topics that elicit a wide range of arguments and perspectives. Here are some common arguments related to agriculture and food:

Food Security: Supporters of modern agriculture argue that conventional farming practices, such as the use of synthetic fertilizers and pesticides, genetic modification, and intensive animal farming, are necessary to meet the growing global demand for food. They contend that these practices maximize crop yields, increase food production, and ensure food security for a growing population.

Sustainable Agriculture: Advocates for sustainable agriculture argue for practices that minimize environmental impact, protect natural resources, and promote long-term sustainability. They emphasize organic farming methods, agroecology, regenerative agriculture, and permaculture as ways to preserve soil health, biodiversity, and ecosystem resilience.

Environmental Impact: Critics of conventional agriculture highlight the negative environmental consequences associated with certain farming practices. They point to the pollution of water bodies from runoff, soil erosion, habitat destruction, deforestation, greenhouse gas emissions, and the loss of biodiversity. They argue that transitioning to more sustainable farming methods can help mitigate these impacts.

Health and Nutrition: Arguments related to health and nutrition revolve around the impact of different agricultural practices on human well-being. Some argue that industrial agriculture, with its reliance on synthetic inputs and monoculture, leads to nutrient-poor food and may contribute to health issues. Supporters of organic and sustainable agriculture claim that these methods can produce healthier and more nutritious food.

Animal Welfare: Animal rights activists and supporters argue for improved animal welfare standards in the agricultural industry. They call for more humane treatment of animals, advocating for animal welfare regulations, reduced confinement, access to outdoor spaces, and better slaughter practices.

Local and Sustainable Food Systems: Advocates for

local and sustainable food systems argue for a shift away from centralized, industrialized food production and towards locally sourced and sustainable food. They emphasize the benefits of shorter supply chains, reduced food miles, support for local farmers, and the promotion of diverse and healthy diets.

Economic Viability and Farming Communities: Discussions on agriculture and food often touch upon the economic viability of farming and rural communities. Supporters argue for fair pricing, access to markets, and policies that support small-scale and family farmers. They emphasize the importance of maintaining vibrant rural communities and the social fabric they contribute to.

Food Waste and Distribution: Arguments related to food waste highlight the inefficiencies in the food system, from production to consumption. Supporters argue for measures to reduce food waste, improve distribution networks, and address food insecurity through better management of surplus food.

Genetic Modification and Biotechnology: Arguments surrounding genetically modified organisms (GMOs) and biotechnology in agriculture are often contentious. Supporters argue that GMOs can increase crop yields, enhance nutritional value, and improve resistance to pests, diseases, and climate change. Critics express concerns about potential environmental risks, health impacts, corporate control of the food system, and the lack of long-term studies on GMO safety.

It's important to note that the agricultural and food landscape is complex, and different regions, contexts, and perspectives may influence the arguments and discussions surrounding it. Engaging in constructive dialogue, considering multiple viewpoints, and finding a balance between productivity, sustainability, health, and social considerations are essential for addressing the challenges and shaping the future of agriculture and food production.

Achieving sustainable agriculture and food systems is crucial for ensuring food security, reducing environmental impacts, and promoting the well-being of both people and the planet. Here are some key strategies to foster sustainability in agriculture and food systems:

Regenerative and organic farming: Encourage the adoption of regenerative agricultural practices that promote soil health, biodiversity, and natural ecosystem functions. Organic farming methods reduce the use of synthetic chemicals, minimize soil erosion, and enhance ecosystem resilience.

Efficient water management: Implement water-efficient irrigation systems, such as drip irrigation or precision irrigation, to minimize water use and reduce water waste. Employing water-saving techniques like mulching and improving soil water retention also contribute to sustainable water management.

Crop diversification and rotation: Promote the practice of crop diversification and rotation to improve soil fertility, control pests and diseases, and reduce the reliance on chemical inputs. Crop diversity also enhances ecosystem resilience and provides habitat for beneficial insects and wildlife.

Sustainable pest and disease management: Utilize integrated pest management (IPM) approaches that combine biological, cultural, and chemical control methods to manage pests and diseases effectively while minimizing the use of synthetic pesticides. This approach reduces chemical exposure, protects beneficial organisms, and preserves ecosystem balance.

Agroforestry and conservation practices: Integrate trees, shrubs, and other perennial plants into agricultural landscapes to provide multiple benefits, such as soil conservation, carbon sequestration, biodiversity support, and enhanced water quality.

Reduce food waste: Implement measures to reduce food waste throughout the supply chain, from production to consumption. This includes better harvesting practices, improved storage and transportation, and consumer education about mindful consumption.

Sustainable livestock management: Promote sustainable practices in animal agriculture, such as providing adequate space for animals, improving feed efficiency, managing manure to minimize pollution, and considering alternative protein sources like plant-based alternatives.

Support local and sustainable food systems: Encourage the development of local and regional food systems that prioritize small-scale farmers, reduce food miles, and promote community resilience. Support farmers' markets, community-supported agriculture (CSA), and farm-to-table initiatives.

Sustainable fishing and aquaculture: Promote sustainable fishing practices that minimize bycatch, protect endangered species, and respect marine ecosystems. Encourage responsible aquaculture practices that prioritize animal welfare, water quality, and minimize ecological impacts.

Policy support and incentives: Governments can play a vital role in promoting sustainable agriculture through policies, regulations, and incentives. This includes providing financial support, research funding, and implementing agricultural practices that prioritize sustainability.

While sustainable agriculture and food systems offer numerous benefits, several obstacles and challenges need to be addressed for their widespread adoption. Some of the key obstacles include:

Limited awareness and knowledge: Many farmers and stakeholders may have limited awareness of sustainable agricultural practices and their benefits. Lack of knowledge and understanding about sustainable techniques, such as organic farming or agroecology, can hinder their adoption.

Economic viability and profitability: Transitioning to sustainable agriculture may require upfront investments, changes in farming practices, and potential yield fluctuations. Farmers may face challenges in accessing financial resources, markets, and receiving fair prices for sustainably produced goods.

Access to resources and technology: Small-scale farmers, especially in developing regions, may face challenges in accessing resources such as land, water, seeds, and agricultural inputs. Limited access to sustainable technologies and equipment can also hinder the adoption of sustainable practices.

Policy and regulatory barriers: Inadequate policies, regulations, and incentives may impede the transition to sustainable agriculture. Lack of supportive policies or inconsistent regulations can discourage farmers from adopting sustainable practices and hinder the development of sustainable food systems.

Market demand and consumer preferences: Consumer demand for sustainable and locally produced food is growing, but challenges remain in creating consistent and robust markets for sustainably produced goods. Educating consumers about the benefits of sustainable agriculture and encouraging them to make conscious food choices is essential.

Scale and scalability: Scaling up sustainable agriculture practices to meet global food demand can be challenging. Ensuring that sustainable practices can be implemented effectively at a larger scale while maintaining their environmental and social benefits requires careful planning, research, and collaboration.

Climate change and weather variability: Climate change poses significant challenges to sustainable agriculture. Erratic weather patterns, increased pests and diseases, and water scarcity can affect crop yields and productivity. Building resilience through climate-smart agricultural practices and adaptation strategies is essential.

Knowledge transfer and capacity building: Disseminating knowledge and providing training on sustainable agriculture practices to farmers, extension workers, and relevant stakeholders is crucial. Accessible and effective extension services and capacity-building programs can support the adoption and implementation of sustainable practices.

Complex supply chains and food systems: Transforming food systems to be more sustainable involves multiple stakeholders, complex supply chains, and coordination across sectors. Aligning the interests and actions of farmers, processors, retailers, policymakers, and consumers is a challenge that requires collaboration and systemic changes.

Cultural and behavioral factors: Traditional farming practices, cultural norms, and resistance to change can be barriers to adopting sustainable agriculture. Overcoming ingrained practices and promoting a shift towards sustainable approaches may require cultural sensitivity and tailored communication strategies.

Addressing these obstacles requires a multi-dimensional approach involving governments, policymakers, farmers, consumers, researchers, and civil society. It involves creating supportive policies, providing financial incentives, fostering knowledge transfer and capacity building, and promoting market mechanisms that reward sustainable practices. Collaboration and partnership among stakeholders are vital for overcoming these obstacles and achieving widespread adoption of sustainable agriculture and food systems. By adopting these strategies and promoting sustainable agriculture and food systems, we can reduce environmental impacts, preserve natural resources, enhance food security, and support the well-being of communities and ecosystems.

~ 21 ~

WATER

Water is a critical resource, and discussions surrounding water management and allocation can generate various arguments and perspectives. Here are some common arguments related to water:

Access to Clean Water: Supporters argue that access to clean and safe drinking water is a fundamental human right. They emphasize the importance of providing equitable access to clean water for all individuals and communities, particularly in regions where water scarcity or water pollution is prevalent.

Water Scarcity and Conservation: Arguments related to water scarcity highlight the need for responsible water use and conservation practices. Supporters emphasize the importance of reducing water waste, implementing efficient irrigation techniques in agriculture, and promoting water-saving technologies to ensure sustainable water supplies for both present and future generations.

Water and Economic Development: Water plays a crucial role in economic development and various industries. Supporters argue that reliable and sufficient water supplies are essential for agriculture, manufacturing, energy production, and other economic activities. They stress the need for balanced water allocation to support economic growth while considering environmental sustainability.

Ecosystem Protection: Discussions around water often involve arguments for protecting aquatic ecosystems, rivers, lakes, and wetlands. Advocates emphasize the ecological value of these habitats, as they provide vital ecosystem services, support biodiversity, and contribute to water quality and overall ecosystem health. They argue for sustainable water management practices that prioritize ecological needs.

Water Pollution and Quality: Concerns about water pollution arise in discussions on water management. Supporters emphasize the importance of reducing industrial, agricultural, and domestic pollution to safeguard water quality. They argue for stricter regulations, pollution control measures, and improved wastewater treatment systems to protect human health and the environment.

Water Rights and Allocation: Water rights and allocation can be contentious issues, particularly in regions where water resources are limited. Arguments may revolve around equitable distribution, prioritizing water for basic human needs, supporting agricultural livelihoods, or balancing water needs for different sectors, such as industry and environmental conservation.

Transboundary Water Management: Water resources shared between different countries or regions often give rise to arguments over transboundary water management. Discussions may involve negotiations, agreements, and conflicts surrounding the equitable allocation, use, and governance of shared water bodies.

Climate Change and Water: The impacts of climate change on water resources are significant. Arguments may center around adapting to changing water availability, managing droughts and floods, and mitigating climate change to minimize its effects on water supplies and associated challenges.

Privatization of Water: Arguments arise over the privatization of water utilities and services. Supporters argue that private sector involvement can improve efficiency, investment, and service delivery. Critics express concerns about affordability, access, and the potential for profit-driven approaches to compromise equitable water access.

Polluted water can have severe consequences on human health, leading to various water-related disasters. Here are some examples of the impacts of polluted water on human populations:

Waterborne Diseases: Contaminated water is a major cause of waterborne diseases. Pathogens such as bacteria, viruses, and parasites can enter water sources through sewage, industrial waste, or agricultural runoff. When people consume or come into contact with contaminated water, they can contract diseases such as cholera, typhoid fever, dysentery, hepatitis A, and giardiasis. These diseases can cause severe diarrhea, dehydration, organ damage, and in some cases, death.

Chemical Contamination: Industrial activities, improper waste disposal, and agricultural runoff can introduce various toxic chemicals and pollutants into water sources. These contaminants may include heavy metals, pesticides, fertilizers, pharmaceuticals, and industrial chemicals. Ingesting or being exposed to these chemicals through contaminated water can lead to a range of health problems, including organ damage, developmental issues, neurological disorders, and even cancer.

Harmful Algal Blooms: Excessive nutrient pollution, often caused by runoff from agricultural or urban areas, can lead to harmful algal blooms in water bodies. These blooms can release toxins harmful to human health. When people come into contact with or consume water contaminated with these toxins, they can experience symptoms such as skin rashes, respiratory issues, gastrointestinal problems, and in severe cases, liver damage or neurological effects.

Contaminated Groundwater: Pollutants can seep into groundwater, which is a significant source of drinking water for many communities. Contamination of groundwater can occur from various sources, including improper waste disposal, industrial activities, and leaking underground storage tanks. Consuming groundwater contaminated with pollutants such as arsenic, nitrates, or volatile organic compounds can have serious health impacts, including increased cancer risks, organ damage, and developmental issues.

Disasters and Contaminated Water Supply: Natural disasters like floods, hurricanes, or earthquakes can disrupt water infrastructure and lead to contamination of water supplies. Floodwaters can carry a wide range of pollutants, including sewage, chemicals, and debris, contaminating drinking water sources. This can result in outbreaks of waterborne diseases and exacerbate the health risks faced by affected populations.

To prevent and mitigate the impacts of polluted water on human health, it is essential to implement effective water treatment and sanitation systems, improve water quality monitoring, promote proper waste management practices, and raise awareness about the importance of clean water and hygiene. Additionally, implementing regulations and policies to control pollution sources and promote sustainable water management is crucial in reducing the occurrence of polluted water disasters on humans.

Water resource management plays a critical role in protecting our planet's water ecosystems, ensuring water availability for human needs, and mitigating the impacts of water-related challenges such as water scarcity, pollution, and climate change. Clean water is essential for the health and functioning of our planet in several ways:

Ecosystem Support: Clean water is vital for the health and integrity of aquatic ecosystems, including rivers, lakes, wetlands, and oceans. These ecosystems provide habitats for countless species, support biodiversity, and facilitate various ecological processes. Clean water supports the growth of aquatic plants, algae, and phytoplankton, forming the base of the food chain and sustaining aquatic life.

Drinking Water: Clean water is a fundamental requirement for human health and well-being. Access to safe and clean drinking water is crucial to prevent waterborne diseases and maintain hygiene. It is essential for human survival and plays a significant role in reducing child mortality rates and improving overall health outcomes.

Agriculture and Food Production: Clean water is necessary for irrigation, livestock watering, and agricultural processes. Sustainable access to clean water supports crop growth, ensuring food security and the livelihoods of farming communities. It is a critical resource for maintaining agricultural productivity and sustainable food production systems.

Industry and Economic Activities: Numerous industries and economic sectors rely on clean water for their operations. Water is used in manufacturing, energy production, mining, and other industrial processes. Access to clean water is essential for economic growth, job creation, and the functioning of various industries.

Biodiversity Conservation: Many terrestrial species also depend on clean water sources for their survival. Rivers and streams provide habitat for a wide range of plants and animals, including migratory species. Wetlands are crucial ecosystems that rely on clean water to support unique biodiversity and provide important services such as water filtration and flood regulation.

Climate Regulation: Water plays a role in the global climate system. Through processes such as evaporation, precipitation, and transpiration from plants, water helps regulate temperature, moisture, and humidity in the atmosphere. This, in turn, influences weather patterns and helps maintain the stability of regional and global climates.

It is important to conserve and protect clean water sources through responsible water management, pollution control, and sustainable practices. Safeguarding clean water contributes to the overall health of ecosystems, human well-being, economic prosperity, and the preservation of biodiversity. Here are key strategies for effective water resource management:

Sustainable water use: Promote water conservation and efficiency measures in households, industries, and agriculture. Encourage the use of water-saving technologies, such as efficient irrigation systems, leak detection, and water-efficient appliances.

Watershed management: Adopt integrated watershed management approaches to protect water sources and maintain the health of ecosystems. This involves land use planning, reforestation, erosion control, and maintaining riparian buffers to prevent pollution and ensure water quality.

Water infrastructure and storage: Develop and maintain water infrastructure, including reservoirs, dams, and canals, to store and distribute water efficiently. Implement appropriate water storage and management systems to cope with variations in water availability and optimize water use.

Water quality protection: Implement measures to

prevent water pollution from point sources (e.g., industrial discharges) and non-point sources (e.g., agricultural runoff). Promote the use of sustainable practices
and technologies to minimize the release of pollutants
into water bodies.

The Cuyahoga River Fire of 1969 is often associated with
Lake Erie, as the river flows into the lake. The Cuyahoga
River, located in Ohio, experienced multiple fires over the
years due to industrial pollution and the presence of flam-
mable materials in the water. The most well-known fire
occurred on June 22, 1969, when an oil slick on the river's
surface ignited, resulting in flames and smoke visible from
the shoreline.

The Cuyahoga River Fire of 1969 was a significant event
in the history of environmental activism in the United
States. It drew national attention to the issue of water
pollution and played a role in shaping the subsequent
environmental regulations and the establishment of the
Environmental Protection Agency (EPA).

Since then, substantial efforts have been made to improve water quality in Lake Erie and the Cuyahoga River.
The implementation of stricter environmental regulations, pollution control measures, and the cleanup of industrial waste have significantly reduced pollution levels
and minimized the occurrence of such incidents. Today,
Lake Erie is known for its ongoing challenges related
to harmful algal blooms, nutrient pollution, and other

environmental issues, but the situation has improved compared to the past.

Ecosystem conservation and restoration: Protect and restore wetlands, rivers, and other water ecosystems to maintain biodiversity and support ecological functions. Healthy ecosystems help regulate water flow, improve water quality, and provide habitats for aquatic life.

Integrated water resources management: Adopt an integrated and holistic approach to water management, considering the interconnectedness of water systems, land use, and socio-economic factors. This involves stakeholder engagement, coordinated planning, and the integration of water management with other sectors such as agriculture, energy, and urban planning.

Climate change adaptation: Develop strategies to adapt to the impacts of climate change on water resources, such as changes in precipitation patterns, increased frequency of droughts, and rising sea levels. This may include water storage and conservation measures, groundwater management, and enhancing water resilience in infrastructure and ecosystems.

Education and awareness: Promote water literacy and raise public awareness about the importance of water conservation, pollution prevention, and sustainable water management practices. Encourage individuals and communities to adopt water-saving behaviors and participate in local water management initiatives.

Collaboration and governance: Foster collaboration among government agencies, communities, private sectors, and civil society organizations to ensure effective water governance. Establish clear roles and responsibilities, develop robust policies and regulations, and promote participatory decision-making processes.

International cooperation: Encourage international cooperation and dialogue to address transboundary water issues, sharing of best practices, and jointly managing shared water resources. Collaboration among countries can lead to more sustainable and equitable water management.

By implementing these strategies, we can safeguard water resources, maintain healthy water ecosystems, and meet the needs of present and future generations while protecting our planet's water resources.

Water resource management faces several challenges that can hinder its effectiveness. Some of the key challenges include:

Water scarcity and increasing demand: Growing population, urbanization, and industrialization contribute to increased water demand, while climate change exacerbates water scarcity in many regions. Balancing water supply and demand becomes a significant challenge, particularly in areas with limited freshwater resources.

Water pollution and degradation: Pollution from industrial discharges, agricultural runoff, inadequate sanitation systems, and improper waste disposal contaminates water bodies. Addressing water pollution requires robust monitoring systems, effective regulations, and widespread adoption of pollution prevention measures.

Inadequate infrastructure and aging systems: Many regions face challenges related to aging water infrastructure, inadequate storage capacity, and inefficient distribution systems. Upgrading and maintaining infrastructure requires substantial investment and long-term planning.

Lack of integrated approach: Fragmented water governance and management can hinder effective water resource management. The lack of coordination among various stakeholders, including government agencies, communities, and industries, can result in conflicting priorities and inefficient use of water resources.

Transboundary water management: Shared water resources across international borders pose challenges in terms of cooperation, equitable distribution, and management. Disputes and conflicts over water rights and allocation can arise, requiring effective international agreements and collaboration.

Climate change impacts: Climate change leads to altered precipitation patterns, increased frequency of extreme weather events, and rising sea levels, affecting water availability and quality. Adapting to climate change and building resilience in water resource management is a complex and ongoing challenge.

Socio-economic disparities: Access to safe and reliable water services is often unequal, with marginalized communities disproportionately affected by water scarcity, poor water quality, and lack of sanitation facilities. Ensuring equitable access to water resources and addressing social and economic disparities is a crucial challenge.

Financial constraints: Adequate funding for water resource management is often a challenge, particularly in developing countries. Lack of financial resources can hinder infrastructure development, monitoring and enforcement efforts, and investment in sustainable water management practices.

Data and information gaps: Insufficient data on water availability, water use, and water quality can limit effective decision-making in water resource management. Improving data collection, monitoring systems, and information sharing is essential for informed and evidence-based management.

Public awareness and stakeholder engagement: Engaging communities and stakeholders in water management decisions and promoting public awareness about water issues can be challenging. Building public support for sustainable water management practices and behavior change requires effective communication and education efforts.

Addressing these challenges requires integrated approaches, strong governance frameworks, collaboration among stakeholders, and long-term planning. It also involves investing in water infrastructure, adopting sustainable water management practices, and promoting awareness and behavior change at the individual and community levels.

Individuals can play a crucial role in managing water resources by adopting responsible and sustainable practices. Here are some actions individuals can take to contribute to water resource management:

Conserve water: Practice water conservation by being mindful of your water usage. Simple steps like turning off the tap while brushing your teeth, fixing leaky faucets promptly, and using water-efficient appliances can significantly reduce water wastage.

Collect rainwater: Install rain barrels or other rainwater harvesting systems to collect and store rainwater. This water can be used for gardening, irrigation, or other non-potable purposes, reducing the strain on municipal water supplies.

Landscape wisely: Choose native or drought-resistant plants for your landscaping, as they require less water to thrive. Mulch your garden beds to retain moisture and minimize evaporation. Use irrigation systems that deliver water directly to the plants' roots, such as drip irrigation, rather than sprinklers.

Practice responsible irrigation: If you have a lawn or garden, water during cooler parts of the day, such as early morning or evening, to minimize evaporation. Avoid overwatering by monitoring soil moisture levels and adjusting watering frequency accordingly.

Be mindful of household practices: Opt for water-efficient appliances and fixtures, such as low-flow toilets and showerheads. Run the dishwasher and washing machine with full loads to maximize water efficiency. Reuse graywater (e.g., from showers or laundry) for non-potable purposes like flushing toilets or watering plants (where permitted).

Avoid water pollution: Properly dispose of hazardous substances, chemicals, and pharmaceuticals to prevent water contamination. Opt for environmentally friendly cleaning products and avoid excessive use of fertilizers and pesticides, which can seep into groundwater.

Educate yourself and others: Stay informed about water-related issues in your area and educate yourself on water conservation and sustainable practices. Share your knowledge with family, friends, and neighbors to raise awareness and encourage responsible water use.

Participate in community initiatives: Join local water conservation programs or community organizations working towards sustainable water management. Engage in river clean-up events or participate in local water conservation campaigns to make a collective impact.

Remember, while individual actions are essential, comprehensive water resource management also requires concerted efforts from governments, communities, and industries.

The choice between tap water and bottled water depends on various factors, including the quality, cost, convenience, and environmental impact. Here are some considerations when comparing tap water and bottled water:

Quality: In many developed countries, tap water is strictly regulated and subject to rigorous testing to ensure it meets safety standards. Municipal water treatment facilities employ processes to remove contaminants and ensure the water is safe to drink. Bottled water is also regulated, but standards may vary depending on the country. It's important to check the source and quality of bottled water before purchasing.

Cost: Tap water is generally more cost-effective than bottled water. The price of tap water typically includes the cost of treatment, distribution, and infrastructure maintenance, which is usually lower than purchasing bottled water regularly. Bottled water, on the other hand, can be significantly more expensive, especially when consumed in large quantities.

Convenience: Tap water is readily available in most homes, workplaces, and public spaces. It can be easily accessed by turning on a faucet or drinking fountain. Bottled water provides convenience when traveling or in areas where access to clean tap water is limited. However, relying solely on bottled water can be less convenient in terms of purchasing, carrying, and disposing of the bottles.

Environmental impact: Bottled water has a significant environmental footprint. The production, transportation, and disposal of plastic bottles contribute to pollution and energy consumption. Plastic bottles often end up in landfills or as litter, taking hundreds of years to decompose. In contrast, tap water has a lower environmental impact as it doesn't require single-use packaging.

Taste and preferences: Personal taste preferences can influence the choice between tap water and bottled water. Some people may prefer the taste of bottled water or find it more consistent. However, taste can vary based on regional differences in tap water sources and treatment methods.

Considering these factors, many experts recommend prioritizing tap water as the primary source of drinking water due to its safety, cost-effectiveness, and lower environmental impact. However, there may be situations where bottled water is necessary or preferred, such as when traveling to areas with compromised water quality or during emergencies.

Regardless of the choice, it's important to stay hydrated and make sustainable choices. If tap water quality concerns exist, using water filters or purifiers can be an option to enhance the taste and further ensure water safety.

GLOBAL WARMING AND CLIMATE CHANGE MITIGATION

Climate change is a highly debated and complex topic, and there are various arguments and perspectives surrounding it. Here are some common arguments related to climate change:

Scientific Consensus: The overwhelming majority of climate scientists agree that human activities, particularly the burning of fossil fuels and deforestation, are the primary drivers of the current climate change. They argue that the increasing concentration of greenhouse gases in the atmosphere is causing global warming and related impacts, such as rising temperatures, sea-level rise, and extreme weather events.

Skepticism and Denial: Some individuals and groups argue against the scientific consensus on climate change. Climate change skeptics or deniers often question the extent of human influence on climate, argue that natural factors are responsible for observed changes, or assert that the science is not yet settled. Skepticism may arise from political, economic, or ideological motivations, or from a lack of trust in scientific institutions.

Economic Considerations: Critics of climate change mitigation measures raise concerns about the potential economic impacts. They argue that transitioning to cleaner energy sources and implementing climate policies could lead to job losses in certain industries, increased energy costs, and hinder economic growth. Some argue for a focus on economic development and poverty alleviation rather than immediate climate action.

Technological Solutions: Some argue that technological advancements and innovation can address climate change. They advocate for investment in renewable energy, energy efficiency, and carbon capture and storage technologies as solutions to reduce greenhouse gas emissions. They believe that market-driven innovation and adaptation will be more effective than government regulations or international agreements.

Interests of Fossil Fuel Industry: Critics argue that climate change skepticism or denial is fueled by vested interests, particularly from fossil fuel industries. They claim that these industries may financially support misinformation campaigns, lobby against climate policies, or create doubt around climate science to protect their profits and influence public opinion.

Adaptation versus Mitigation: Another argument revolves around the balance between adaptation and mitigation strategies. Some argue that instead of focusing solely on reducing greenhouse gas emissions, resources should be directed towards adapting to the changing climate and building resilience to its impacts. They claim that adaptation measures can be more practical, cost-effective, and beneficial in the short term.

It's important to note that the overwhelming scientific consensus supports the reality of human-induced climate change. However, public discourse often includes a wide range of opinions and perspectives. It is crucial to engage in constructive dialogue, rely on credible scientific information, and consider the long-term consequences of climate change when discussing this complex and pressing global issue.

Global warming, also referred to as climate change, presents several challenges that need to be addressed urgently. Here are some of the key challenges associated with global warming:

Rising Temperatures: The Earth's average temperature is increasing due to the buildup of greenhouse gases in the atmosphere, primarily carbon dioxide from human activities. Rising temperatures lead to numerous consequences, including more frequent and severe heatwaves, changing weather patterns, and shifts in ecosystems.

Extreme Weather Events: Global warming is linked to an increase in extreme weather events such as hurricanes, droughts, floods, and wildfires. These events can cause significant damage to infrastructure, homes, and ecosystems, leading to human displacement, economic losses, and loss of lives.

Sea-Level Rise: As global temperatures rise, glaciers and ice caps melt, causing sea levels to rise. This poses a significant threat to coastal communities, low-lying areas, and small island nations. Rising sea levels increase the risk of coastal erosion, saltwater intrusion into freshwater sources, and flooding during storms.

Disruption of Ecosystems: Global warming impacts ecosystems and biodiversity. Changes in temperature and precipitation patterns can disrupt habitats, alter migration patterns, and affect the survival of various plant and animal species. This disruption can lead to loss of biodiversity and ecosystem services, affecting human well-being.

Food and Water Security: Global warming has implications for food production and water resources.

Changing weather patterns, including droughts and floods, can negatively impact crop yields and agricultural productivity. Additionally, shifts in rainfall patterns can affect water availability and quality, leading to water scarcity and threatening food security in many regions.

Public Health Risks: Global warming can have adverse effects on human health. Heatwaves can increase the risk of heat-related illnesses and deaths. Changes in the distribution of vector-borne diseases, such as malaria and dengue fever, can also occur as changing temperatures and rainfall patterns influence the habitats of disease-carrying insects.

Socioeconomic Impacts: Global warming can exacerbate existing social and economic inequalities. Vulnerable communities, including those in low-income regions and developing countries, often have limited resources to adapt to and cope with the impacts of climate change. Disruptions in agriculture, infrastructure, and economic sectors can lead to increased poverty and social instability.

Climate change mitigation refers to efforts and actions taken to reduce or prevent the emission of greenhouse gases (GHGs) into the atmosphere and to minimize the impact of human activities on climate change. Mitigation strategies aim to limit global warming, reduce the severity of climate change impacts, and transition towards a low-carbon and sustainable future. Here are some key areas of climate change mitigation:

Transition to renewable energy: Shifting away from fossil fuels and increasing the use of renewable energy sources such as solar, wind, hydro, and geothermal power can significantly reduce GHG emissions associated with electricity generation and other sectors.

Energy efficiency: Improving energy efficiency in buildings, transportation, and industrial processes reduces energy consumption and associated emissions. This includes initiatives like energy-efficient appliances, insulation, public transportation, and sustainable urban planning.

Forest conservation and reforestation: Protecting existing forests and restoring degraded areas help sequester carbon dioxide (CO_2) and preserve biodiversity. Forests act as carbon sinks, absorbing CO_2 from the atmosphere, and mitigating climate change.

Sustainable transportation: Encouraging the use of low-carbon transportation options such as electric vehicles, public transportation, cycling, and walking reduces emissions from the transportation sector, a significant contributor to GHG emissions.

Sustainable agriculture: Promoting sustainable farming practices, such as agroecology, precision agriculture, and organic farming, can reduce emissions from agricultural activities and improve soil health and carbon sequestration.

Waste management: Implementing waste reduction, recycling, and composting programs can help minimize methane emissions from landfills. Additionally, recovering energy from waste through anaerobic digestion or waste-to-energy facilities can contribute to renewable energy generation.

Industry and manufacturing: Implementing energy-efficient technologies, improving industrial processes, and adopting cleaner production methods can reduce emissions from manufacturing and industrial sectors.

Carbon pricing and policy interventions: Implementing carbon pricing mechanisms, such as carbon taxes or cap-and-trade systems, can create economic incentives for reducing emissions and promoting cleaner technologies.

Research and development: Investing in research and development of low-carbon technologies, sustainable practices, and innovative solutions can accelerate the transition to a low-carbon economy.

International cooperation: Encouraging global collaboration and agreements, such as the Paris Agreement, to collectively address climate change and mitigate its impacts on a global scale.

It is essential to implement a combination of these strategies and continue to innovate and adapt as new opportunities and technologies emerge. Climate change mitigation requires collective efforts from governments, businesses, communities, and individuals to achieve significant and long-lasting results. But climate change mitigation faces various obstacles that can hinder its progress. These obstacles include:

Political challenges: Climate change mitigation requires strong political will and international cooperation. However, differing priorities, competing interests, and challenges in reaching consensus among nations can hinder the implementation of effective climate policies and agreements.

Economic considerations: Transitioning to low-carbon technologies and sustainable practices may require significant upfront investments. The perceived short-term costs and potential economic impacts can create resistance or hesitation from businesses, industries, and governments.

Technological barriers: The development and deployment of low-carbon technologies at scale face challenges such as high costs, technological limitations, and the need for infrastructure upgrades. Research and development efforts are necessary to overcome these barriers and make clean technologies more accessible and affordable.

Limited public awareness and understanding: Climate change is a complex issue, and public understanding and awareness can vary. Lack of knowledge, misconceptions, and skepticism can hinder support for climate change mitigation efforts and policy implementation.

Socio-political dynamics and vested interests: Certain industries and stakeholders may have vested interests in maintaining the status quo, particularly those heavily reliant on fossil fuels. Resistance to change and lobbying efforts can impede progress in implementing effective mitigation measures.

Inequality and social justice concerns: Climate change impacts and mitigation efforts can exacerbate existing social and economic inequalities. Vulnerable communities, particularly in developing countries, often face the greatest risks from climate change but may have limited resources and capacity to adapt or mitigate its impacts.

Financing and resource limitations: Adequate financial resources and technology transfer are necessary to support climate change mitigation efforts, especially in developing countries. Limited access to funding, lack of financial mechanisms, and technological barriers can hinder progress, particularly for the most vulnerable regions.

Policy and regulatory challenges: Inconsistent or inadequate policies, weak enforcement, and regulatory gaps can hinder effective climate change mitigation. Clear and consistent policies, supportive regulatory frameworks, and strong governance structures are essential for successful implementation.

Uncertainty and long-term planning: Climate change involves complex and interconnected systems with uncertainties in predicting future impacts and understanding the effectiveness of mitigation measures. Long-term planning and decision-making are required, but uncertainties can pose challenges in setting appropriate targets and strategies.

Resistance to behavioral change: Addressing climate change requires changes in individual and collective behaviors, such as reducing energy consumption, adopting sustainable practices, and making environmentally conscious choices. Resistance to behavioral change and the inertia associated with established habits can impede progress.

Addressing these challenges requires a comprehensive approach that includes mitigation efforts to reduce greenhouse gas emissions and adaptation strategies to build resilience to the impacts of global warming. It requires a multi-faceted approach that addresses economic, social, technological, and political dimensions to foster a collective response to the challenges. This involves transitioning to renewable energy sources, improving energy efficiency, promoting sustainable land use practices, enhancing climate resilience in infrastructure, and supporting international cooperation and climate policies at the global level. Additionally, raising awareness, education, and community engagement are crucial for fostering individual and collective action to address global warming challenges.

~ 23 ~

ENERGY

Arguments over energy resources stem from differing viewpoints on the best approaches to meet energy needs, environmental impacts, economic considerations, and technological feasibility. Here are some common arguments related to energy resources:

Fossil Fuels and Energy Security: Supporters of fossil fuels argue that they have historically been reliable and affordable sources of energy, providing a stable energy supply and supporting economic growth. They emphasize the existing infrastructure and the ability of fossil fuels to meet high energy demands, especially during peak periods. Additionally, they may highlight the importance of energy independence and national security associated with domestic fossil fuel production.

Climate Change and Renewable Energy: Advocates for renewable energy argue that transitioning away from fossil fuels is necessary to mitigate climate change. They emphasize the urgency of reducing greenhouse gas emissions and the benefits of clean energy sources such as solar, wind, and hydropower. They highlight the potential for renewable energy to decarbonize the energy sector and reduce dependence on finite fossil fuel resources.

Environmental Impacts: Discussions surrounding energy resources often involve arguments about their environmental impacts. Critics of fossil fuels highlight air pollution, water contamination, habitat destruction, and the contribution of greenhouse gas emissions to climate change. Supporters of renewable energy emphasize that clean energy sources have fewer adverse environmental effects, such as reduced carbon emissions and minimal air and water pollution.

Cost and Affordability: Arguments over energy resources often revolve around cost considerations. Supporters of fossil fuels argue that they remain cost-effective and provide reliable energy at a lower price. They may express concerns about the affordability and intermittency of renewable energy sources. Supporters of renewables argue that the costs of renewable energy technologies have been decreasing, making them increasingly competitive and economically viable in the long run.

Energy Independence and Job Creation: Discussions

may focus on the economic aspects of energy resources. Supporters of fossil fuels may emphasize the potential for job creation in the industry and argue that reliance on domestic fossil fuel resources enhances energy independence. Advocates for renewable energy contend that investing in clean energy technologies can stimulate economic growth, create jobs, and promote innovation in emerging industries.

Nuclear Power: Arguments related to energy resources often involve discussions about nuclear power. Supporters argue that nuclear power provides a reliable and low-carbon source of energy, capable of meeting significant energy demands. They highlight its potential as a baseload power source and its contribution to reducing greenhouse gas emissions. Critics express concerns about safety risks, radioactive waste disposal, and the potential for accidents or nuclear proliferation.

Technological Feasibility and Innovation: Discussions surrounding energy resources often consider the feasibility of different technologies. Supporters of fossil fuels argue that the existing infrastructure and technology associated with these resources make them more practical and reliable. Supporters of renewable energy assert that technological advancements, innovation, and research and development can address challenges associated with intermittency, storage, and grid integration, making renewable energy sources more viable.

Community and Public Health: Arguments over energy resources may touch upon community and public health considerations. Critics of fossil fuels may highlight the health risks associated with air pollution, particularly in areas near power plants or extraction sites. They argue that transitioning to cleaner energy sources can improve public health outcomes and reduce healthcare costs.

It's important to note that regional contexts, political perspectives, and local energy resources can influence the specific arguments surrounding energy resources. Engaging in informed and respectful discussions, considering multiple factors, and balancing the social, environmental, and economic aspects are essential for shaping the future energy landscape.

Polluted energy refers to energy sources and processes that produce harmful pollutants and contribute to environmental degradation. The effects of polluted energy can have wide-ranging impacts on human health, ecosystems, and the overall environment. Here are some key effects of polluted energy:

Air Pollution: The combustion of fossil fuels, such as coal, oil, and natural gas, for energy production releases pollutants into the air, including sulfur dioxide

(SO$_2$), nitrogen oxides (NOx), particulate matter (PM), and greenhouse gases like carbon dioxide (CO$_2$). These pollutants contribute to air pollution, leading to respiratory problems, cardiovascular diseases, and other health issues in humans. They also contribute to smog formation and the deterioration of air quality, impacting ecosystems and harming vegetation.

Climate Change: Polluted energy sources, particularly those that emit high levels of greenhouse gases, contribute to climate change. Increased concentrations of greenhouse gases in the atmosphere trap heat and lead to global warming. This results in rising temperatures, altered weather patterns, sea-level rise, and the melting of ice caps and glaciers. Climate change has far-reaching consequences for ecosystems, agriculture, water resources, and human livelihoods.

Water Pollution: Polluted energy production and processes can contaminate water bodies through various means. For instance, the disposal of coal ash or mining waste can leach toxic substances into nearby water sources. Oil spills and leaks from oil and gas extraction and transportation can contaminate rivers, lakes, and oceans. These pollutants can harm aquatic life, disrupt ecosystems, and compromise the availability of clean water for human consumption.

Land Degradation: Extracting and mining fossil fuels can lead to land degradation, habitat destruction, and deforestation. Mountaintop removal coal mining, for example, alters landscapes and destroys ecosystems. The construction and operation of polluting energy infrastructure, such as coal mines and oil refineries, can have detrimental effects on local biodiversity and natural habitats.

Health Impacts: Polluted energy sources and associated pollutants have direct health impacts on nearby communities. Exposure to air pollutants like sulfur dioxide, nitrogen oxides, and particulate matter can lead to respiratory problems, cardiovascular diseases, lung cancer, and other health issues. Additionally, the extraction and transportation of fossil fuels can pose occupational health risks for workers involved in these industries.

Environmental Disasters: Certain forms of polluted energy production, such as offshore drilling or mining accidents, can result in major environmental disasters. Oil spills, gas leaks, or nuclear accidents can cause extensive damage to ecosystems, marine life, and natural habitats. These disasters can take years or even decades to recover from and have long-lasting environmental and economic consequences.

To mitigate the effects of polluted energy, transitioning to cleaner and renewable energy sources is crucial. Increasing the use of renewable energy technologies like solar power, wind power, hydropower, and geothermal energy can help reduce air pollution, mitigate climate change, and promote sustainable development. Additionally, improving energy efficiency, implementing stricter emissions regulations, and promoting sustainable practices in energy production and consumption are essential steps toward a cleaner and healthier energy future.

Climate-friendly energy refers to forms of energy production and consumption that have minimal or no negative impact on the climate and contribute to reducing greenhouse gas emissions. Here are some examples of climate-friendly energy sources:

Renewable energy: Renewable energy sources derive their power from natural processes that are constantly replenished and do not deplete natural resources. They have low or zero carbon dioxide emissions during operation. Examples include:

Solar power: Generated by converting sunlight into electricity using photovoltaic (PV) panels.

Wind power: Generated by harnessing the kinetic energy of wind to rotate wind turbines and produce electricity.

Hydropower: Generated by harnessing the energy of flowing water, such as rivers and dams, to generate electricity.

Geothermal energy: Utilizes the natural heat from

within the Earth to generate electricity or provide direct heating and cooling.

Biomass energy: Generated by converting organic materials, such as crop residues, wood, and agricultural waste, into heat or electricity.

Nuclear power: While controversial due to safety concerns and waste management issues, nuclear power is a low-carbon energy source. Nuclear power plants generate electricity by splitting atoms (nuclear fission), which releases significant amounts of energy. However, the use of nuclear power is subject to strict regulatory controls and requires proper waste disposal.

Energy efficiency: Energy efficiency involves reducing the amount of energy required to perform a specific task or provide a service. By using energy-efficient appliances, improving insulation, adopting efficient transportation systems, and implementing energy management practices, we can minimize energy waste and reduce greenhouse gas emissions.

Carbon capture and storage (CCS): CCS technologies aim to capture carbon dioxide emissions from power plants and industrial facilities and store them underground or utilize them in other applications. While CCS does not directly produce energy, it can help reduce the carbon footprint of existing fossil fuel-based power plants and industrial processes.

Sustainable transportation: Transitioning to low-carbon transportation is crucial for addressing climate change. Electric vehicles (EVs), powered by electricity from renewable sources, produce zero tailpipe emissions. Additionally, public transportation systems, cycling, and walking can reduce the reliance on fossil fuel-powered vehicles.

Smart grids and energy storage: Implementing smart grid technologies and energy storage systems allows for better integration of renewable energy sources and improved management of electricity demand. These technologies enable the storage of excess energy generated from renewable sources and its efficient distribution during peak demand periods.

Green hydrogen: Hydrogen produced through electrolysis using renewable energy sources (green hydrogen) has the potential to replace fossil fuels in various sectors, such as transportation and industry. It can be used as a clean fuel or as an energy carrier for storage and conversion.

Transitioning to climate-friendly energy sources is crucial for mitigating climate change and achieving sustainability goals. It requires a combination of policy support, technological advancements, and behavioral changes to promote the adoption of these cleaner alternatives.

~ 24 ~

SOLAR POWER

Solar power refers to the generation of electricity or heat using energy from the sun. It is a form of renewable energy that harnesses the sun's radiation and converts it into usable energy through various technologies.

Overview of solar power:

Photovoltaic (PV) Systems: Photovoltaic systems, commonly known as solar panels, convert sunlight directly into electricity. Solar panels are made up of multiple solar cells, typically composed of silicon or other semiconducting materials. When sunlight hits the solar cells, it creates an electric current through the photovoltaic effect. The electricity generated by the solar panels can be used immediately or stored in batteries for later use.

Solar Thermal Systems: Solar thermal systems capture the sun's heat to produce hot water, space heating, or generate steam for electricity production. This technology utilizes solar collectors, such as flat-plate collectors or evacuated tube collectors, to absorb and transfer the sun's heat to a fluid (usually water or a heat-transfer fluid). The heated fluid can be used directly or stored for later use.

Concentrated Solar Power (CSP): Concentrated solar power systems use mirrors or lenses to concentrate sunlight onto a receiver, which converts the solar energy into heat. This heat is then used to generate electricity by driving a turbine. CSP technologies include parabolic troughs, power towers, and dish Stirling systems.

Challenges associated with solar power include the intermittency of sunlight, as solar energy generation is dependent on weather conditions and daylight hours. However, advancements in energy storage technologies, such as batteries, are addressing this challenge by enabling the storage of excess energy for use during periods of low sunlight.

Overall, solar power is a rapidly growing and increasingly important source of clean and sustainable energy, playing a significant role in transitioning to a more sustainable and low-carbon energy future.

Building and collecting solar power involves several key components and considerations. Here are the main aspects involved in harnessing solar energy:

Photovoltaic (PV) Panels: Solar panels, also known as photovoltaic (PV) panels, are the primary component for collecting solar power. These panels consist of multiple solar cells made of semiconducting materials, typically silicon, which convert sunlight directly into electricity through the photovoltaic effect.

Mounting Systems: Solar panels need to be securely mounted and positioned to maximize sun exposure. Mounting systems can vary depending on the installation type, such as rooftop, ground-mounted, or solar farms. They include structures, frames, and racks that hold the panels in place and allow for tilt and orientation adjustments.

Inverters: The electricity generated by solar panels is in direct current (DC) form, but most household and commercial electrical systems operate on alternating current (AC). Inverters are used to convert the DC electricity produced by the solar panels into AC electricity compatible with the electrical grid or for use in buildings.

Electrical Wiring and Connections: Proper electrical wiring and connections are essential for the safe and efficient operation of a solar power system. This includes wiring the solar panels together in series or parallel configurations, connecting the panels to the inverter, and integrating the system with the building's electrical system or the grid.

Mounting and Balance of System Components: Apart from panels, solar power systems require other balance of system (BOS) components. These include junction boxes, combiner boxes, wiring conduits, circuit breakers, fuses, disconnect switches, and other electrical and safety equipment. These components are necessary for system protection, monitoring, and efficient operation.

Solar Charge Controllers and Battery Systems (Optional): In off-grid or hybrid solar systems, solar charge controllers and battery systems are used to store excess electricity generated during the day for use during periods of low or no sunlight. These components are crucial for providing power when the sun is not available or during power outages.

Solar Monitoring Systems: Solar monitoring systems enable the tracking and analysis of solar energy production and system performance. These systems can provide real-time data on electricity generation, system efficiency, and potential issues, helping optimize performance and identify maintenance needs.

Permitting and Installation: Installing a solar power system often requires obtaining permits and complying with local regulations and building codes. This includes ensuring proper electrical and structural safety, adherence to zoning requirements, and coordination with utility companies for grid connection and net metering agreements.

Maintenance and Operation: Regular maintenance is necessary to ensure optimal performance and longevity of the solar power system. This includes cleaning the panels, inspecting electrical connections, monitoring system performance, and addressing any issues or repairs as needed.

It's important to consider the specific requirements and considerations for each solar project, as they can vary depending on factors such as the size of the system, location, solar resource availability, and intended purpose (grid-connected or off-grid). Engaging qualified solar professionals, such as solar installers and electricians, is recommended for the design, installation, and maintenance of solar power systems.

Arguments over solar power often revolve around its benefits, limitations, and considerations. Here are some common arguments related to solar power:

Renewable and Clean Energy: Advocates for solar power highlight its status as a renewable energy source that generates electricity from sunlight. They argue that solar power offers a clean and sustainable alternative to fossil fuels, producing no greenhouse gas emissions or air pollutants during operation.

Climate Change Mitigation: Supporters of solar power emphasize its role in mitigating climate change. They argue that widespread adoption of solar energy can significantly reduce greenhouse gas emissions and help transition to a low-carbon economy, contributing to global efforts to limit global warming and its associated impacts.

Energy Independence and Security: Arguments in favor of solar power often center around energy independence. Supporters argue that harnessing solar energy locally reduces dependence on imported fossil fuels, enhancing energy security and resilience. They highlight the potential for distributed solar installations to empower communities and individuals to generate their own clean electricity.

Job Creation and Economic Benefits: Advocates assert that solar power can stimulate economic growth and create job opportunities. They highlight the potential for solar power projects to generate employment in manufacturing, installation, maintenance, and related sectors. Additionally, they argue that solar power investments can attract private capital and spur innovation, benefiting local economies.

Cost Competitiveness and Affordability: Supporters of solar power argue that the cost of solar energy has significantly decreased over the years, making it increasingly competitive with conventional energy sources. They highlight the potential for long-term cost savings, as solar power systems have no fuel costs and can provide electricity over decades with minimal maintenance.

Intermittency and Energy Storage: Critics of solar power often raise concerns about its intermittency, as solar energy generation depends on sunlight availability. They argue that solar power requires energy storage solutions or backup power sources to ensure continuous electricity supply. Critics may also highlight the challenges of grid integration and managing fluctuations in solar power output.

Land Use and Environmental Impact: Arguments over solar power may involve discussions about land use and potential environmental impacts. Critics express concerns about the need for large land areas for utility-scale solar installations, which can impact natural habitats and agricultural land. They argue for careful site selection, land-use planning, and consideration of environmental implications in solar project development.

Aesthetics and Visual Impact: Discussions around solar power sometimes touch upon the visual impact of solar panels, particularly in residential areas or scenic landscapes. Critics argue that the appearance of solar installations can affect property values or disrupt visual aesthetics. Supporters argue for innovative design and integration techniques to minimize visual impacts.

Government Support and Policy: Arguments over solar power often involve discussions about government support and policies. Supporters advocate for incentives, subsidies, and favorable regulations that promote solar power deployment, research, and development. Critics may question the cost-effectiveness of government support programs and express concerns about market distortions.

It's important to note that specific arguments can vary depending on factors such as geographic location, energy policies, grid infrastructure, and public perception. Engaging in informed discussions, considering local contexts, and weighing the benefits and challenges of solar power are crucial for developing sustainable and effective energy strategies.

Solar power offers numerous benefits as a renewable energy source. Here are some key advantages of solar power:

Renewable and Sustainable: Solar power harnesses energy from the sun, which is an abundant and inexhaustible resource. As long as the sun continues to shine, solar energy can be collected and utilized, making it a sustainable and renewable energy option.

Reduced Greenhouse Gas Emissions: Solar power generation produces minimal greenhouse gas emissions compared to fossil fuel-based power sources. By using solar energy, we can significantly reduce carbon dioxide (CO_2) and other harmful pollutants, helping mitigate climate change and improve air quality.

Energy Independence: Solar power allows for greater energy independence by reducing reliance on traditional energy sources, such as fossil fuels. Generating electricity from solar energy can help diversify the energy mix, decrease dependence on imported energy, and enhance energy security.

Lower Operating Costs: Once a solar power system is installed, the sunlight used for electricity generation is free. This can lead to significant savings on electricity bills over the system's lifespan, especially in areas with high electricity costs. Solar panels also have minimal operating and maintenance costs.

Scalability and Modularity: Solar power systems can be tailored to meet different energy needs, from small-scale residential installations to large-scale solar farms. The modularity of solar panels allows for easy expansion and addition of capacity as energy requirements grow.

Job Creation and Economic Benefits: The solar industry has the potential to create jobs and stimulate economic growth. Solar power projects require skilled workers for manufacturing, installation, maintenance, and operation. Investing in solar energy can contribute to local job creation, support small businesses, and attract investment in the renewable energy sector.

Remote Power Generation: Solar power is particularly advantageous in remote areas or regions with limited access to electricity grids. It provides a reliable and sustainable energy source for off-grid communities, powering homes, schools, clinics, and other critical facilities.

Long Lifespan and Durability: Solar panels are designed to withstand various weather conditions and have a long lifespan. They can operate efficiently for 25 to 30 years or more with proper maintenance. This durability ensures a long-term and reliable energy source.

Community Resilience: Distributed solar power systems, such as rooftop solar panels, promote community resilience by decentralizing energy production. This reduces the vulnerability to power outages and grid failures, allowing communities to maintain access to electricity during emergencies.

Environmental Benefits: Solar power has several environmental benefits. It helps reduce air and water pollution associated with conventional energy sources, minimizes the use of water resources for cooling, and avoids the environmental impacts of extracting and transporting fossil fuels.

As solar technology continues to advance and costs decline, the benefits of solar power become increasingly attractive for individuals, businesses, and governments looking to transition to cleaner and more sustainable energy solutions.

While solar power has numerous environmental and economic benefits, there are some downsides associated with its implementation. Here are a few potential downsides of solar power:

Intermittency and variability: Solar power generation depends on the availability of sunlight, which varies throughout the day and is absent during nighttime and adverse weather conditions. This intermittency can pose challenges for meeting electricity demands consistently, especially without energy storage systems or backup power sources.

Land and space requirements: Solar photovoltaic (PV) systems require significant land or rooftop space to install enough solar panels. Large-scale solar installations may encroach upon natural habitats, agricultural land, or open spaces, potentially impacting biodiversity, and land use.

Manufacturing and disposal impacts: The production of solar panels involves the use of various materials, including silicon, metals, and chemicals. The extraction, manufacturing, and disposal processes can generate waste, consume energy, and potentially result in environmental pollution if not properly managed.

Cost and affordability: While the cost of solar panels has decreased significantly over the years, the initial installation costs can still be relatively high. The affordability of solar power systems may pose a barrier to widespread adoption, particularly in economically disadvantaged communities or regions with limited financial incentives and support.

Transmission and grid integration: Solar power plants are often located in regions with abundant sunlight, which may be far from the areas of high electricity demand. Transmitting the electricity over long distances can result in transmission losses and necessitates a well-developed grid infrastructure for efficient integration.

Environmental impacts during production: The production of solar panels and other components may generate greenhouse gas emissions, especially if the manufacturing processes rely on fossil fuel-based energy sources. Additionally, the extraction of raw materials and the disposal of old or damaged panels can have environmental implications if not managed properly.

Large-scale solar installations, such as solar farms, can alter the visual landscape and may face opposition due to aesthetic concerns. Balancing the need for clean energy with community preferences and environmental considerations is important in the planning and implementation of solar projects.

Despite these downsides, the overall environmental benefits of solar power, such as reduced greenhouse gas emissions and decreased reliance on fossil fuels, often outweigh the challenges. Ongoing research and technological advancements aim to address these concerns and further improve the efficiency, cost-effectiveness, and sustainability of solar energy systems.

Purposed solution to land and space requirements to avoid deforestation and encroach upon natural habitats and agricultural land; this process is already being done in some areas but why not across the board. Utilized parking lots and raise the solar panels high enough to avoid possible hazards; this is already being accomplished, but not in that many States.

Some benefits:

Money maker for landowners.

Pedestrians/automobiles are protected from the elements.

Could provide energy to charging station for electric autos.

Utilization of already established wide open spaces.

Reduction in ecosystem disruption.

Solar power is generally considered a safe and environmentally friendly form of renewable energy. However, like any other form of energy production, there is a potential for accidents or incidents. It is important to note that major disasters specifically related to solar power installations are rare. Here are a few examples of incidents that have occurred:

Fire incidents: While solar panels themselves do not pose a significant fire risk, there have been cases where solar installations have caught fire due to electrical faults or other factors. These incidents are relatively uncommon but can occur if there are issues with wiring, faulty equipment, or improper installation. It's worth mentioning that the risk of fire can be minimized through adherence to proper installation standards, regular maintenance, and the use of high-quality equipment.

Chemical exposure during manufacturing: The production of solar panels involves the use of various chemicals and materials. Improper handling or inadequate safety measures in the manufacturing process can lead to worker exposure to potentially hazardous substances. Stringent safety protocols and proper disposal practices are essential to mitigate these risks.

It is crucial to emphasize that these incidents are exceptional cases, and the overall safety record of solar power installations is very good. Solar power is considered a low-risk energy source compared to conventional fossil fuel-based power generation. It does not produce greenhouse gas emissions during operation, contributes to energy independence, and has minimal environmental impact.

Proper installation, regular maintenance, and adherence to safety regulations and guidelines are essential to ensure the safe and efficient operation of solar power systems. Ongoing advancements in technology, as well as robust industry standards and regulations, continue to enhance the safety and reliability of solar power as a sustainable energy solution.

~ 25 ~

WIND POWER

Wind power is a form of renewable energy that harnesses the kinetic energy of the wind to generate electricity. It involves converting the motion of the wind into mechanical energy, which is then converted into electrical energy through the use of wind turbines.

Here's how wind power works:

Wind Turbines: Wind turbines are large structures with multiple blades mounted on a tower. The blades are designed to capture the energy from the wind as it flows past them. Modern wind turbines are typically made of lightweight and durable materials such as fiberglass or carbon fiber.

Wind Energy Conversion: When the wind blows, it causes the turbine blades to rotate. The rotation of the blades turns a shaft connected to a generator, which converts the mechanical energy into electrical energy.

Electrical Grid Integration: The electricity generated by wind turbines is typically transmitted through power lines and integrated into the electrical grid. It can be used to power homes, businesses, and industries, or stored in batteries for later use.

Challenges associated with wind power include the intermittency of wind, as wind speeds can vary, and turbines generate electricity only when the wind is blowing within a certain range. However, grid integration strategies, energy storage technologies, and a diverse energy mix can help address this challenge.

Overall, wind power plays a crucial role in the transition to a more sustainable and low-carbon energy future, contributing to reducing greenhouse gas emissions, fostering energy independence, and promoting economic development.

Arguments over wind power often revolve around its benefits, drawbacks, and considerations. Here are some common arguments related to wind power:

Renewable and Clean Energy: Supporters of wind power emphasize its status as a renewable energy source that harnesses the power of wind to generate electricity. They argue that wind power offers a clean and sustainable alternative to fossil fuels, producing no greenhouse gas emissions or air pollutants during operation.

Climate Change Mitigation: Advocates for wind power highlight its role in mitigating climate change. They argue that widespread adoption of wind energy can significantly reduce greenhouse gas emissions and help transition to a low-carbon economy, contributing to global efforts to limit global warming and its associated impacts.

Energy Independence and Security: Arguments in favor of wind power often center around energy independence. Supporters argue that harnessing wind energy locally reduces dependence on imported fossil fuels, enhancing energy security and resilience. They highlight the potential for domestic wind resources to provide a stable and abundant source of clean electricity.

Job Creation and Economic Benefits: Advocates assert that wind power can stimulate economic growth and create job opportunities. They highlight the potential for wind power projects to generate employment in manufacturing, installation, maintenance, and related sectors. Additionally, they argue that wind power investments can attract private capital and contribute to local economic development.

Cost Competitiveness and Affordability: Supporters of wind power argue that the cost of wind energy has significantly decreased over the years, making it increasingly competitive with conventional energy sources. They highlight the potential for long-term cost savings, as wind power systems have no fuel costs and can provide electricity over decades with proper maintenance.

Intermittency and Grid Integration: Critics of wind power often raise concerns about its intermittency, as wind energy generation depends on wind availability. They argue that wind power requires backup power sources or energy storage solutions to ensure continuous electricity supply. Critics may also highlight challenges related to grid integration, transmission infrastructure, and managing fluctuations in wind power output.

Land Use and Environmental Impact: Arguments over wind power may involve discussions about land use and potential environmental impacts. Critics express concerns about the visual impact of wind turbines, noise pollution, and potential effects on wildlife and bird populations. Supporters argue that proper siting, environmental assessments, and design considerations can minimize these impacts.

Aesthetics and Local Community Concerns: Discussions surrounding wind power sometimes touch upon aesthetics and community concerns. Critics argue that wind turbines can disrupt scenic landscapes, affect property values, or generate noise that may impact local communities. Supporters highlight the benefits of community engagement, transparent decision-making processes, and economic opportunities for local residents through wind power projects.

Government Support and Policy: Arguments over wind power often involve discussions about government support and policies. Supporters advocate for incentives, subsidies, and favorable regulations that promote wind power deployment, research, and development. Critics may question the cost-effectiveness of government support programs and express concerns about potential market distortions.

It's important to note that specific arguments can vary depending on factors such as geographic location, energy policies, wind resources, and public perception. Engaging in informed discussions, considering local contexts, and weighing the benefits and challenges of wind power are crucial for developing sustainable and effective energy strategies.

To harness wind power and generate electricity, several key components and processes are involved. Here are the main aspects of making wind power:

Wind Turbines: Wind turbines are the primary equipment used to capture the kinetic energy of the wind and convert it into electrical energy. These tall structures consist of rotor blades, a hub, and a nacelle (housing the gearbox, generator, and control systems). The size and design of wind turbines can vary depending on the specific project and desired power output.

The disposal of wind turbine rotor blades is an important consideration in the lifecycle of wind power projects. Here are some common approaches to handling wind turbine rotor blade disposal:

Recycling: Recycling is an increasingly common method for managing wind turbine rotor blades at the end of their operational life. Blades are typically made of composite materials, such as fiberglass reinforced with resin. Recycling involves processes to separate and recover the different materials, such as fiberglass, resin, and other components. These materials can then be used in various applications, such as construction materials, automotive parts, or even in the manufacturing of new blades.

Landfill: In some cases, wind turbine rotor blades may be sent to landfill facilities for disposal. However, due to their size and composition, blades take up significant space in landfills. Efforts are being made to reduce the amount of waste going to landfills and explore alternative disposal options.

Incineration: Incineration, or energy recovery through combustion, is another method that can be used to dispose of wind turbine rotor blades. Blades can be incinerated at high temperatures, and the resulting heat can be used to generate energy. However, incineration may raise concerns about emissions and the potential release of pollutants.

Repurposing and Upcycling: Some organizations and researchers are exploring creative ways to repurpose or upcycle retired wind turbine rotor blades. This includes transforming them into architectural structures, artworks, furniture, or other functional objects. These initiatives help reduce waste and give the blades a new purpose.

It's worth noting that the disposal of wind turbine rotor blades is a relatively new challenge, as the first generation of wind turbines installed decades ago is now reaching the end of their operational life. As the wind energy industry continues to grow and mature, efforts are being made to develop more sustainable and environmentally friendly solutions for rotor blade disposal. Research and innovation are focused on improving the recyclability of blade materials, exploring new recycling technologies, and finding innovative uses for retired blades.

Regulations and best practices regarding wind turbine rotor blade disposal may vary by region. Local authorities, wind industry organizations, and manufacturers are actively working on developing guidelines and policies to address this issue in a responsible and environmentally conscious manner.

Wind Resource Assessment: Assessing the wind resource at a particular site is crucial to determine the feasibility and potential energy output of a wind power project. This involves collecting wind speed and direction data over an extended period to analyze the wind patterns, turbulence, and variability in the area.

Site Selection: Identifying suitable locations with consistent and strong wind resources is essential for the success of a wind power project. Factors such as average wind speed, wind direction, topography, land availability, proximity to electrical grids, and potential environmental impacts are considered during site selection.

Infrastructure and Grid Connection: Developing wind power projects requires establishing the necessary infrastructure. This includes constructing access roads, installing power collection systems (underground cables or overhead lines), and establishing a connection to the electrical grid for transmitting the generated electricity.

Wind Farm Layout and Turbine Installation: The layout of wind turbines within a wind farm is carefully planned to optimize energy capture and minimize turbulence caused by neighboring turbines. Turbines are erected using cranes and specialized equipment, securely anchored to the ground, and connected to the power collection system.

Operations and Maintenance: Wind turbines require regular operations and maintenance activities to ensure optimal performance and reliability. This includes inspections, cleaning, lubrication, component replacements, and troubleshooting. Advanced monitoring systems and remote diagnostics are often employed to detect and address issues promptly.

Energy Storage and Grid Integration: Integrating wind power into the electrical grid involves managing fluctuations in power output due to variations in wind speed. Energy storage systems, such as batteries, can help store excess electricity during periods of high generation and release it during low wind periods or peak demand times. Grid integration strategies, such as smart grid technologies and demand response programs, are implemented to balance supply and demand.

Environmental and Social Considerations: Assessing and addressing potential environmental and social impacts is a crucial aspect of wind power development. This includes conducting environmental impact assessments, considering wildlife and habitat protection measures, engaging with local communities, and addressing potential noise or visual concerns.

Financing and Policy Support: Wind power projects often require significant upfront investment. Securing financing through public or private sources, along with supportive policies and incentives, can help make wind power economically viable and attractive to investors.

Monitoring and Performance Evaluation: Continuous monitoring and performance evaluation of wind turbines and wind farms are conducted to assess energy production, identify maintenance needs, optimize operations, and ensure compliance with regulatory standards.

Developing wind power projects requires expertise in engineering, project management, environmental assessment, and electrical systems. Collaboration between various stakeholders, including project developers, engineers, researchers, governments, and local communities, is crucial for successful wind power implementation.

Wind power offers several advantages as a renewable energy source. Here are some key advantages of wind power:

Clean and Renewable: Wind power is a clean and renewable energy source that does not produce greenhouse gas emissions or air pollutants during operation.

It helps reduce reliance on fossil fuels and mitigates climate change.

Abundant Resource: Wind is a widely available resource that can be harnessed in various locations around the world. Wind turbines can be installed onshore, offshore, or in distributed settings, making it a versatile energy option.

Energy Independence: Wind power provides energy independence by diversifying the energy mix and reducing dependence on imported fuels. It contributes to greater energy security and resilience.

Low Operating Costs: Once a wind turbine is installed, the cost of generating electricity from wind power is relatively low. The fuel source (wind) is free, and ongoing operating and maintenance costs are generally low compared to conventional power plants.

Job Creation and Economic Benefits: The wind power sector creates jobs and stimulates local economies. It requires skilled workers for manufacturing, installation, maintenance, and operation. Investments in wind power can attract private investments, support local businesses, and contribute to regional economic growth.

Scalability and Modularity: Wind power projects can range from small-scale installations to large wind farms with multiple turbines. They can be scaled up or down depending on energy needs, making wind power flexible and adaptable to different requirements.

Public Health Benefits: Wind power generation does not produce air pollutants, such as sulfur dioxide, nitrogen oxides, or particulate matter, which are associated with negative health impacts. By reducing reliance on fossil fuel combustion, wind power contributes to improved air quality and public health.

Land Multipurpose Use: Wind turbines occupy a relatively small footprint, allowing land underneath and around them to be used for multiple purposes, such as agriculture, grazing, or recreation. This enables the co-existence of wind power projects with other land uses.

Rapid Deployment: Wind power projects can be deployed relatively quickly compared to traditional power plants, such as coal or nuclear plants. Once the necessary infrastructure is in place, wind turbines can be constructed and commissioned in a relatively short timeframe.

Technological Advancements: Advances in wind turbine technology, including larger turbines, improved efficiency, and enhanced energy storage systems, continue to increase the potential of wind power as a reliable and cost-effective energy source.

While wind power offers numerous advantages, it is important to consider factors such as wind resource availability, potential impacts on wildlife and ecosystems, community acceptance, and grid integration when planning wind power projects. Effective siting, environmental assessments, and stakeholder engagement are crucial for maximizing the benefits of wind power while minimizing potential drawbacks.

While wind power has significant advantages as a renewable energy source, it also has a few downsides to consider. Here are some of the potential downsides of wind power:

Visual and aesthetic impact: Wind turbines, especially when installed in large numbers, can alter the visual landscape and scenic views. Some people find the presence of wind turbines unsightly, leading to concerns about the visual impact on natural and cultural landscapes.

Noise and health concerns: Wind turbines can produce low-frequency noise and vibrations during operation. While modern wind turbines are designed to minimize noise, the proximity of turbines to residential areas can still lead to complaints about noise pollution. Additionally, some individuals have reported health concerns, such as sleep disturbances and headaches, which are attributed to living near wind farms. However, scientific studies have generally found no direct causal link between wind turbines and adverse health effects.

Bird and bat mortality: Wind turbines can pose a risk to birds and bats, particularly in areas where migratory routes or important habitats overlap with wind farm locations. Collisions with turbine blades or changes in local wind patterns caused by turbines can result in bird and bat fatalities. However, compared to other human-related factors such as buildings, communication towers, and power lines, wind turbines contribute to a relatively small percentage of bird and bat mortality.

Land and habitat impact: Wind farms require a considerable amount of land to accommodate multiple turbines, access roads, and other associated infrastructure. This land use can potentially impact natural habitats, including wildlife habitats, vegetation, and ecosystems. Careful planning and siting of wind farms can help minimize these impacts and consider ecological sensitivities.

Intermittency and variability: Like solar power, wind power is dependent on weather conditions and is subject to variability and intermittency. Wind speeds can fluctuate, resulting in inconsistent power generation. Therefore, integration with energy storage systems or other complementary energy sources is necessary to ensure a reliable and consistent electricity supply.

Potential impact on radar systems and aviation: Wind turbines can interfere with radar systems, particularly those used for air traffic control or military purposes. This interference can require mitigation measures or careful siting of wind farms to avoid compromising radar capabilities. Additionally, wind turbines can pose obstacles and safety considerations for low-flying aircraft, such as in the vicinity of airports or military training areas.

The disposal of wind turbine blades is a growing concern as the lifespan of wind turbines reaches their end. Currently, there are a few methods for handling wind turbine blade disposal:

Landfill disposal: A common method is to send decommissioned wind turbine blades to landfills. However, this method has environmental drawbacks, as the blades are made of composite materials (usually fiberglass or carbon fiber-reinforced polymers) that do not readily decompose. This results in long-term waste accumulation.

Recycling: Efforts are being made to develop recycling technologies for wind turbine blades. The process involves separating the composite materials into their constituent parts, such as fiberglass and resins, which can be recycled or repurposed. Some companies are exploring options to reuse blades in other industries, like construction materials or as feedstock for cement production.

Thermal decomposition: Another emerging approach is thermal decomposition, which involves using high temperatures to break down the composite materials into their basic components. This method can convert the materials into energy or chemical products, potentially minimizing waste and resource consumption.

Repurposing: Repurposing old wind turbine blades for other uses is being explored. For instance, blades can be cut into smaller sections and used as architectural or design elements, such as in art installations or furniture production. However, repurposing options are limited due to the large size and specific design of wind turbine blades.

It is important to note that the wind energy industry is actively seeking more sustainable and environmentally friendly solutions for wind turbine blade disposal. Research and development efforts are underway to improve recycling technologies and explore innovative methods for managing decommissioned blades effectively. As the industry evolves, it is expected that more efficient and sustainable disposal methods will be developed to reduce waste and minimize environmental impact.

Despite these downsides, wind power remains one

of the most environmentally friendly and cost-effective sources of renewable energy. Continued research and technological advancements aim to address these challenges, improve turbine efficiency, reduce environmental impacts, and enhance the overall acceptance and integration of wind power into the energy mix.

While wind power is generally considered a safe and reliable form of renewable energy, there have been a few notable incidents involving wind turbines. It's important to note that these incidents are rare, and that wind power has a strong safety record overall. Here are a couple of examples:

Ocotillo Wind Farm Blade Failure (California, 2013): In 2013, a wind turbine blade at the Ocotillo Wind Farm in California broke off and fell to the ground, resulting in concerns about safety. The incident led to an investigation to determine the cause, and it was ultimately attributed to a manufacturing defect in the blade. Steps were taken to inspect and repair other turbines in the wind farm to prevent similar occurrences.

Smøla Wind Farm Collision (Norway, 2006): In 2006, a significant number of bird fatalities occurred at the Smøla Wind Farm in Norway. The wind turbines were located in an area with high bird activity, and it was discovered that the rotating blades posed a risk to birds, especially during certain weather conditions and migration periods. Since then, efforts have been made to mitigate the impact on birds, such as adjusting turbine operations during critical periods and implementing measures to improve their visibility.

It's worth noting that the incidents mentioned above are isolated cases, and the wind power industry has implemented various measures to enhance safety and minimize risks. Wind turbine design and construction standards have evolved over time, and ongoing research and technological advancements focus on improving efficiency, reliability, and safety.

When properly sited, maintained, and operated, wind turbines have a minimal environmental impact and are considered one of the cleanest and safest forms of energy generation. The benefits of wind power, including its renewable nature and potential to reduce greenhouse gas emissions, continue to drive its widespread adoption as a sustainable energy source.

~ 26 ~

HYDROPOWER

Hydropower, also known as hydroelectric power, is a renewable energy source that harnesses the energy of flowing or falling water to generate electricity. It is one of the oldest and most widely used forms of renewable energy.

Here's an overview of how hydropower works:

Dam or Diversion Structure: Hydropower plants are typically located near rivers, where a dam or diversion structure is constructed to control the flow of water. A dam creates a reservoir by impounding water, while a diversion structure diverts water from a river into a canal or penstock.

Water Flow: As water is released from the reservoir or diverted into the canal, it flows downhill due to gravity. The force of the flowing or falling water is referred to as the hydraulic head, which is a measure of the potential energy available for conversion into electricity.

Turbines: The flowing water drives a turbine, which is connected to a generator. Turbines convert the kinetic energy of the moving water into mechanical energy. The most common types of turbines used in hydropower plants are Francis, Kaplan, and Pelton turbines, chosen based on the water flow characteristics.

Electricity Generation: As the turbine rotates, it spins the generator, which produces electricity. The electricity generated is then transmitted through power lines to homes, businesses, and industries for consumption.

Hydropower can be categorized into different types:

Conventional Hydropower: Conventional hydropower plants utilize dams to store water in reservoirs and release it as needed to generate electricity. The height of the water column and the flow rate determine the power output.

Run-of-River Hydropower: Run-of-river hydropower systems do not involve large reservoirs. Instead, they divert a portion of the river flow through a canal or penstock to drive turbines. These systems operate based on the natural flow of the river and have a reduced environmental impact compared to large-scale dam projects.

Arguments over hydropower often revolve around its benefits, drawbacks, and considerations. Here are some common arguments related to hydropower:

Renewable Energy and Climate Change Mitigation: Supporters of hydropower emphasize its status as a renewable energy source that utilizes the power of flowing or falling water to generate electricity. They argue that hydropower offers a clean and sustainable alternative to fossil fuels, as it produces no direct greenhouse gas emissions during operation, contributing to efforts to mitigate climate change.

Energy Generation and Reliability: Advocates for hydropower highlight its capacity for large-scale electricity generation. They argue that hydropower provides a stable and reliable source of electricity, capable of meeting high energy demands and contributing to grid stability. They emphasize the ability to control water flows to match electricity demand.

Energy Independence and Security: Arguments in favor of hydropower often center around energy independence. Supporters argue that harnessing domestic water resources reduces dependence on imported fossil fuels, enhancing energy security and resilience. They highlight the potential for hydropower to provide a constant and predictable energy supply.

Baseload Power and Grid Stability: Supporters of hydropower argue that it can serve as a baseload power source, providing a consistent and continuous supply of electricity. They highlight its potential for balancing intermittent renewable energy sources and supporting grid stability, as hydroelectric power plants can quickly adjust generation to meet fluctuations in demand.

Water Resource Management: Supporters assert that hydropower projects provide opportunities for integrated water resource management. They argue that multipurpose reservoirs can offer benefits such as flood control, irrigation, water supply, and recreational opportunities, in addition to electricity generation. They emphasize the potential for coordinated water management to optimize these benefits.

Environmental Impact and Ecological Concerns: Critics of hydropower raise concerns about its environmental impact. They argue that large-scale dams can lead to habitat destruction, alteration of natural river ecosystems, and displacement of communities. Critics also highlight potential impacts on fish migration, water quality, and downstream ecosystems. They advocate for careful assessment and mitigation of these impacts in project planning and operation.

Social and Cultural Considerations: Arguments over hydropower may involve discussions about social and cultural impacts. Critics express concerns about the displacement of local communities, loss of cultural heritage, and the disruption of traditional livelihoods. They emphasize the importance of community engagement, respect for indigenous rights, and equitable distribution of benefits.

Cost, Economics, and Project Viability: Arguments surrounding hydropower may touch upon project economics and viability. Supporters argue that large-scale hydropower projects can provide long-term cost benefits, as they have a long lifespan and low operating costs. Critics may raise concerns about the high upfront costs, environmental mitigation expenses, and potential risks associated with cost overruns.

Alternatives and Distributed Generation: Discussions on hydropower sometimes involve debates about alternative energy sources and distributed generation. Critics argue that decentralized, smaller-scale renewable energy solutions, such as solar and wind power, can offer comparable benefits with fewer environmental and social impacts. They advocate for diversified energy portfolios and exploring a mix of renewable energy sources.

It's important to note that specific arguments can vary depending on factors such as geographic location, project scale, local contexts, and stakeholder perspectives. Engaging in informed discussions, considering diverse viewpoints, and conducting comprehensive assessments are crucial for understanding the benefits and challenges of hydropower and making well-informed decisions.

Building a hydropower project involves several key steps and considerations. Here are the main aspects involved in constructing a hydropower facility:

Feasibility Study: The first step is to conduct a feasibility study to assess the technical, economic, and environmental viability of the hydropower project. This involves evaluating factors such as water availability, topography, potential power generation capacity, environmental impacts, and financial viability.

Site Selection: Identifying a suitable location is crucial for a hydropower project. Factors considered during site selection include water resources, flow characteristics, geology, land availability, proximity to electrical grids, and potential environmental and social impacts.

Permits and Regulatory Approvals: Obtaining the necessary permits and regulatory approvals is essential. This includes complying with environmental regulations, obtaining water rights, and securing permits related to land use, construction, and operation of the hydropower project. The process typically involves coordination with government agencies and local communities.

Engineering and Design: Detailed engineering and design work is carried out to plan the layout and components of the hydropower project. This includes designing the dam (if applicable), water intake structures, powerhouse, turbines, generators, transmission lines, and other infrastructure.

Construction: Construction activities involve various tasks, such as clearing and preparing the site, excavating foundations, constructing dams or weirs (if required), installing penstocks (pipes that carry water to turbines), building the powerhouse, and installing turbines, generators, and other equipment. Construction also includes the installation of transmission lines and substations for connecting the hydropower project to the electrical grid.

Environmental and Social Considerations: During construction, measures are taken to minimize environmental and social impacts. This may involve implementing erosion and sediment control measures, managing construction waste, implementing wildlife protection measures, and addressing potential impacts on local communities and indigenous populations.

Testing and Commissioning: Once construction is complete, thorough testing and commissioning of the hydropower plant are carried out. This includes testing the turbines, generators, control systems, and other equipment to ensure they are functioning properly and meeting performance specifications.

Operation and Maintenance: After commissioning, the hydropower plant enters the operational phase. Regular operation and maintenance activities are conducted to ensure the reliable and efficient functioning of the plant. This includes monitoring water flow, maintaining and inspecting equipment, conducting repairs and replacements as needed, and managing sedimentation.

Grid Connection and Power Distribution: The hydropower plant is connected to the electrical grid to distribute the generated electricity. This involves establishing transmission lines, substations, and other infrastructure to transmit power to end-users.

Monitoring and Compliance: Continuous monitoring and compliance with regulatory requirements are necessary throughout the operation of the hydropower project. This includes monitoring environmental impacts, water quality, fish passage, and compliance with operating licenses and environmental permits.

Hydropower projects require expertise in civil engineering, electrical engineering, environmental sciences, and project management. Collaboration with stakeholders, including government agencies, local communities, and environmental organizations, is crucial for the successful development of a hydropower facility.

Hydropower, or hydroelectric power, offers several advantages as a renewable energy source. Here are some key upsides to hydropower:

Renewable and Clean Energy: Hydropower utilizes the energy of flowing or falling water to generate electricity. It is a renewable energy source as long as there is a consistent water supply, such as a river or reservoir. Hydropower produces minimal greenhouse gas emissions and air pollutants during operation, contributing to cleaner energy generation.

Large-Scale Power Generation: Hydropower plants can generate significant amounts of electricity, ranging from small-scale installations to large hydroelectric dams. The capacity of hydropower plants can be easily adjusted to meet varying energy demands, making it a flexible source of power.

Storage and Dispatchability: Some hydropower systems incorporate reservoirs that can store water. This allows for energy storage, where water can be released when electricity demand is high or renewable energy supply is low. Hydropower plants with storage capabilities can provide dispatchable power, helping stabilize the electrical grid and support intermittent renewable energy sources.

Reliable and Predictable: Hydropower is a reliable source of electricity because water flows can be predicted and controlled. Unlike solar or wind energy, which are subject to weather conditions, hydropower provides a consistent and predictable energy supply, making it a dependable baseload or peaking power source.

Long Lifespan: Hydropower infrastructure, such as dams and turbines, has a long operational life, typically spanning several decades. With proper maintenance and upgrades, hydropower plants can operate efficiently for 50 years or more. This longevity contributes to long-term energy generation and stability.

Flood Control and Water Management: Hydropower projects, especially dams, can help regulate water flow and provide flood control in rivers. They can store excess water during periods of high precipitation and release it gradually during drier periods, reducing the risk of floods downstream. Hydropower facilities can also support water management for irrigation, domestic water supply, and industrial use.

Water Supply and Irrigation: Hydropower projects can provide water resources for various purposes, including irrigation for agriculture. By regulating water flow, hydropower facilities can ensure a consistent water supply for irrigation, enhancing agricultural productivity and water resource management.

Job Creation and Local Economy: Developing and operating hydropower projects can create employment opportunities, both during construction and ongoing maintenance. The projects require skilled workers for engineering, construction, operation, and maintenance activities. Additionally, hydropower projects can stimulate local economies by attracting investments and supporting ancillary industries.

Recreational Opportunities: Hydropower reservoirs and surrounding areas often provide recreational opportunities such as boating, fishing, and tourism. These activities can bring economic benefits to local communities and enhance the overall value of the hydropower project.

Low Operating Costs: Once the initial construction costs are recouped, hydropower generation can have low operating costs compared to fossil fuel-based power plants. The fuel source, water, is essentially free, and ongoing operation and maintenance costs are relatively low.

While hydropower offers numerous advantages, it's important to consider potential environmental and social impacts associated with large-scale projects, such as the alteration of river ecosystems, displacement of communities, and the loss of habitats. Careful planning, environmental impact assessments, and stakeholder engagement are necessary to mitigate potential drawbacks and maximize the benefits of hydropower.

Hydropower is a widely used and renewable source of energy, but there are certain downsides associated with its implementation. Here are some of the potential downsides of hydropower:

Environmental impact: The construction of large dams and reservoirs required for hydropower projects can result in significant environmental impacts. These impacts include habitat disruption, alteration of natural river flow patterns, and the submergence of land and forests. The creation of reservoirs can also lead to the release of greenhouse gases, particularly methane, from the decomposition of organic matter submerged in the reservoir.

Displacement of communities and ecosystems: The construction of large dams can result in the displacement of communities living in the project area. People may need to be relocated, which can have social and economic consequences. Additionally, the altered river flow and habitat changes caused by dams can disrupt aquatic ecosystems, affecting fish populations, migratory patterns, and the overall ecological balance.

Sedimentation and downstream impacts: Dams can trap sediment that would naturally flow downstream. Over time, this can lead to sediment build-up in reservoirs, which reduces their storage capacity and affects downstream ecosystems. The reduced sediment flow can negatively impact riverbanks, coastal areas, and estuaries that rely on a regular supply of sediment for erosion control and maintaining biodiversity.

Altered river ecosystems: The construction of dams and the alteration of river flows can disrupt the natural ecological processes of rivers. This includes changes in water temperature, dissolved oxygen levels, and nutrient distribution, which can impact aquatic plant and animal species, including fish migration and reproduction patterns.

Risk of dam failure: Large dams carry the risk of failure, which can have catastrophic consequences downstream. While dam safety measures are implemented, the possibility of failure due to natural disasters, human error, or technical issues remains a concern.

The biggest dam failure in history is considered to be the failure of the Banqiao Dam in China in 1975. The Banqiao Dam was part of a larger system of dams known as the Shimantan Reservoir Project, located in Henan Province, China.

In August 1975, the region experienced heavy rainfall due to Typhoon Nina. The storm brought exceptionally heavy rainfall that overwhelmed the capacity of the dam system. The Banqiao Dam and more than 60 other dams in the area suffered severe damage and ultimately failed.

The failure of the dams led to catastrophic flooding downstream, affecting an estimated 11 million people. The floods caused widespread devastation, including the collapse of houses, destruction of infrastructure, and loss of crops. The exact death toll from the disaster remains uncertain, with estimates ranging from tens of thousands to over 100,000 people.

The Banqiao Dam failure highlighted the importance of proper design, construction, and maintenance of large dams. It also emphasized the need for effective disaster preparedness and emergency response measures in flood-prone areas. Since then, dam safety standards and practices have been improved and implemented globally to minimize the risk of similar catastrophic failures.

Limited suitable locations: Not all rivers are suitable for hydropower projects due to factors such as size, flow, and environmental sensitivity. Identifying suitable locations with high hydropower potential while minimizing environmental and social impacts can be challenging, particularly in densely populated or environmentally sensitive regions.

Long-term economic viability: While hydropower projects can generate significant amounts of electricity, their long-term economic viability can be influenced by factors such as changing energy markets, environmental regulations, and the need for ongoing maintenance and upgrades.

It is important to assess these potential downsides when planning and implementing hydropower projects. Environmental impact assessments, stakeholder consultations, and considering alternative designs or smaller-scale hydropower systems can help mitigate these downsides and ensure sustainable hydropower development.

A company highly interested in hydropower development for the auto industry is Toyota. Their focus has primarily been on developing and promoting vehicles with lower emissions, including hybrid electric vehicles (HEVs), plug-in hybrid electric vehicles (PHEVs), battery electric vehicles (BEVs), and fuel cell electric vehicles (FCEVs). These technologies aim to reduce dependence on fossil fuels and minimize greenhouse gas emissions. It is worth noting that Toyota continues to investigate and develop hydrogen-powered vehicles. This approach is similar to their previous success with the Prius and initiating a new market of hybrid automobiles.

~ 27 ~

GEOTHERMAL ENERGY

Geothermal energy is a renewable energy source that harnesses the heat stored within the Earth's core. It involves extracting heat from the Earth's interior and converting it into usable energy for various applications. Geothermal energy is considered one of the most reliable and sustainable forms of renewable energy. Here's how geothermal energy works:

Heat Source: The Earth's heat originates from the residual heat from its formation and the radioactive decay of elements within the Earth's core. The temperature increases as you go deeper into the Earth.

Geothermal Reservoirs: Certain regions have higher geothermal heat flow and possess underground reservoirs of hot water and steam known as geothermal reservoirs. These reservoirs are typically found in areas with volcanic activity, tectonic plate boundaries, or geologically active zones.

Geothermal Power Plants: Geothermal power plants tap into these geothermal reservoirs by drilling wells into the hot underground areas. The hot water or steam from the reservoirs is brought to the surface through these wells.

Power Generation: The hot water or steam from the geothermal reservoirs is used to drive turbines connected to generators. The rotating turbines convert the kinetic energy of the steam or water into electrical energy, which can be used to power homes, businesses, and industries.

There are three main types of geothermal power plants:

Dry Steam Power Plants: These plants utilize high-pressure steam from the geothermal reservoirs directly to drive the turbines.

Flash Steam Power Plants: In these plants, high-pressure hot water is pumped from the geothermal reservoirs into a low-pressure tank or separator. The sudden pressure drop causes the water to "flash" into steam, which is then used to power the turbines.

Binary Cycle Power Plants: These plants use the heat from the geothermal reservoirs to heat a fluid with a low boiling point, such as isobutane or isopentane. The heated fluid vaporizes, driving a turbine. The fluid is then condensed and reused in a closed-loop system.

Arguments over geothermal energy often revolve around its benefits, drawbacks, and considerations. Here are some common arguments related to geothermal energy:

Renewable and Clean Energy: Supporters of geothermal energy emphasize its status as a renewable energy source that utilizes the Earth's heat to generate electricity or provide heating and cooling. They argue that geothermal energy offers a continuous and clean alternative to fossil fuels, producing minimal greenhouse gas emissions during operation.

Baseload Power Generation: Advocates for geothermal energy highlight its capacity for baseload power generation. They argue that geothermal power plants can operate continuously, providing a stable and reliable source of electricity. They emphasize the importance of geothermal energy in diversifying the energy mix and reducing reliance on intermittent renewable energy sources.

Energy Independence and Security: Arguments in favor of geothermal energy often center around energy independence. Supporters argue that harnessing local geothermal resources reduces dependence on imported fossil fuels, enhancing energy security and resilience. They highlight the potential for geothermal energy to provide a constant and predictable energy supply.

Environmental Benefits: Supporters of geothermal energy emphasize its low carbon footprint and minimal environmental impact. They argue that geothermal power plants produce significantly lower greenhouse gas emissions compared to fossil fuel-based power plants. They also highlight the absence of fuel combustion, air pollution, or water consumption associated with geothermal energy generation.

Heating and Cooling Applications: Advocates for geothermal energy highlight its applications beyond electricity generation. They argue that geothermal heat pumps can provide efficient heating and cooling for residential, commercial, and industrial buildings. They emphasize the potential for geothermal heating and cooling systems to reduce energy consumption, lower greenhouse gas emissions, and provide long-term cost savings.

Resource Limitations and Site-specific Considerations: Critics of geothermal energy may raise concerns about resource limitations and site-specific considerations. They argue that suitable geothermal resources are geographically constrained and not universally available. Critics may also highlight potential risks such as subsidence, induced seismicity, or water resource depletion associated with certain geothermal energy extraction methods.

High Upfront Costs and Economic Viability: Arguments surrounding geothermal energy may touch upon project economics and viability. Critics may raise concerns about the high upfront costs associated with drilling and infrastructure development for geothermal power plants. They may also question the economic feasibility of geothermal projects compared to other renewable energy sources or conventional fossil fuel-based power generation.

Land Use and Environmental Impact: Discussions over geothermal energy may involve considerations of land use and potential environmental impacts. Critics express concerns about the footprint of geothermal power plants, land disturbance during exploration and drilling, and potential effects on local ecosystems or habitats. They emphasize the importance of careful site selection, environmental assessments, and mitigation measures.

Technological Advancements and Innovation: Supporters argue that ongoing technological advancements and innovation in geothermal energy can improve its efficiency, expand its resource potential, and reduce costs. They highlight the potential for research and development to overcome technical challenges and make geothermal energy more accessible and competitive.

It's important to note that specific arguments can vary depending on factors such as geographic location, resource availability, regulatory frameworks, and stakeholder perspectives. Engaging in informed discussions, considering diverse viewpoints, and conducting comprehensive assessments are crucial for understanding the benefits and challenges of geothermal energy and making well-informed decisions.

Building structures for geothermal energy involves several key components and considerations. Here are some of the important aspects involved in constructing geothermal energy facilities:

Resource Assessment: Before constructing a geothermal power plant, a thorough resource assessment is conducted to determine the quality and quantity of the geothermal resource at the site. This involves studying the geology, subsurface temperatures, and fluid characteristics to ensure the feasibility of the project.

Well Drilling: Geothermal power plants require wells to extract hot water or steam from the underground reservoir. Drilling wells involves specialized equipment and techniques to reach the geothermal resource at the desired depth. Production and injection wells are typically drilled to access the reservoir and create a fluid circulation system.

Power Plant Infrastructure: Geothermal power plants consist of various structures, including powerhouses, turbine buildings, cooling systems, and electrical substations. These structures are designed to accommodate the power generation equipment, such as turbines, generators, heat exchangers, and control systems.

Steam and Water Separation: Hot water or steam extracted from the reservoir contains impurities and may require separation and treatment. Separation systems, such as flash tanks or separators, are employed to separate the steam and remove non-condensable gases and impurities before further processing.

Power Generation Equipment: Geothermal energy can be harnessed through different technologies, including dry steam, flash steam, and binary cycle systems. The choice of power generation technology determines the type of equipment needed, such as turbines, generators, heat exchangers, and condensers, which are used to convert the thermal energy into electricity.

Transmission and Distribution: Geothermal power generated at the plant needs to be transmitted and distributed to consumers. This requires constructing transmission lines, substations, and distribution networks to connect the geothermal facility to the electrical grid and deliver electricity to end-users.

Environmental Considerations: Geothermal projects need to comply with environmental regulations and consider potential impacts on the surrounding ecosystem. Proper management of drilling fluids, control of air emissions, and proper disposal of geothermal brines are some of the environmental considerations during the construction and operation phases.

Infrastructure Support: The construction of geothermal energy facilities requires various support infrastructure, including access roads, water supply systems, and wastewater treatment facilities. These infrastructure components are essential for construction logistics, maintenance activities, and ensuring the sustainable operation of the facility.

Emissions and fluid disposal: While geothermal energy is considered a low-carbon energy source, there can be emissions associated with the extraction and utilization of geothermal fluids. These emissions may include small amounts of greenhouse gases, hydrogen sulfide, and other volatile compounds. Additionally, the disposal of geothermal fluids after energy extraction can require appropriate treatment and management to avoid environmental impacts.

Limited scalability and transmission challenges: Geothermal energy projects are generally limited in scale due to the specific characteristics and availability of geothermal resources. The transmission of geothermal electricity to areas of high demand can also present challenges if the resource is located far from populated regions, requiring significant infrastructure investments.

It's worth noting that the specific requirements and construction processes may vary depending on the type of geothermal resource (e.g., high-temperature resources, low-temperature resources) and the chosen technology for power generation.

Geothermal energy offers several advantages as a renewable energy source. Here are some key advantages of geothermal energy:

Renewable and Sustainable: Geothermal energy is a renewable resource as it draws heat from the Earth's interior, which is continuously replenished by natural processes such as radioactive decay and residual heat from the planet's formation. This means that geothermal energy can be harnessed without depleting finite resources.

Low Greenhouse Gas Emissions: Geothermal energy produces minimal greenhouse gas emissions during the power generation process. Compared to fossil fuel-based power plants, geothermal plants release a significantly lower amount of carbon dioxide (CO_2) and other harmful pollutants into the atmosphere, helping to mitigate climate change and air pollution.

Baseload Power: Geothermal power plants can provide a steady and reliable baseload power supply. Unlike solar and wind energy, which are intermittent sources, geothermal energy can generate electricity consistently, day and night, regardless of weather conditions. This stability contributes to grid reliability and allows for continuous power generation.

High Energy Efficiency: Geothermal power plants have high energy conversion efficiency. They can convert a relatively high proportion of the thermal energy extracted from the Earth into electricity, making them efficient in comparison to some other forms of power generation.

Long Lifespan and Durability: Geothermal power plants have a long lifespan and can operate for several decades with proper maintenance. The underground reservoirs that provide geothermal heat are naturally replenished over time, ensuring a continuous and reliable heat source.

Job Creation and Local Economic Benefits: Developing and operating geothermal energy projects can create jobs and contribute to local economies. The construction, operation, and maintenance of geothermal power plants require a skilled workforce, providing employment opportunities in regions with geothermal resources.

Heat Utilization: Geothermal energy can be utilized not only for electricity generation but also for direct heat applications. Geothermal heat can be used for district heating, space heating, water heating, and various industrial processes, reducing the need for fossil fuel-based heating systems and enhancing energy efficiency.

Smaller Environmental Footprint: Geothermal power plants generally have a smaller physical footprint compared to conventional power plants, such as coal or nuclear plants. They require less land area and can be designed to minimize visual and noise impacts. Additionally, geothermal energy extraction typically does not require large-scale water consumption.

Despite these advantages, it's important to note that geothermal energy is not universally accessible. It requires specific geological conditions and is therefore limited to regions with suitable geothermal resources. However, where these resources are available, geothermal energy can be a valuable and sustainable source of power and heat.

While geothermal energy has several advantages as a renewable energy source, there are a few downsides associated with its utilization. Here are some potential downsides of geothermal energy:

Location limitations: Geothermal energy can only be harnessed in areas with suitable geothermal resources, such as regions with active volcanoes, geothermal reservoirs, or hot springs. This limits the availability of geothermal energy to specific locations, which may not be easily accessible or widespread.

High upfront costs: The initial costs of drilling and constructing geothermal power plants can be substantial. Exploratory drilling to identify suitable geothermal reservoirs and the subsequent installation of wells and infrastructure can require significant investment. These upfront costs can make geothermal projects financially challenging, particularly for smaller-scale or remote applications.

Resource depletion and cooling: Prolonged extraction of geothermal energy from a specific reservoir can lead to the depletion of heat, resulting in a reduction in energy generation over time. The long-term sustainability of a geothermal resource depends on the rate of heat replenishment and careful management of the reservoir to avoid overheating or cooling.

Potential for induced seismic activity: Geothermal operations can sometimes trigger seismic activity, particularly in areas prone to tectonic activity. Injecting water into deep wells for enhanced geothermal systems (EGS) or reinjection of fluids into the reservoir can induce small earthquakes. However, the majority of induced seismic activity associated with geothermal projects is usually minor and not a significant risk.

Geothermal energy harnessing does not typically cause large-scale earthquakes. However, there have been some instances where geothermal activities have been associated with minor seismic events. These induced seismic events are generally of low magnitude and localized, and they are rarely significant or impactful.

One notable example often cited is the Paradox Valley seismic events in Colorado, USA, which occurred in the 1960s. These seismic events were linked to the injection of water for a geothermal energy project. However, the magnitudes of the induced earthquakes were relatively small, ranging from 1.5 to 4.0 on the Richter scale, and they did not cause any significant damage or harm.

It's important to note that proper management and monitoring of geothermal operations can help minimize the risk of induced seismicity. By carefully assessing the geologic conditions, monitoring fluid injection rates and pressures, and adjusting operations as necessary, the potential for induced seismic activity can be effectively managed and controlled.

In general, the seismic risks associated with geothermal

energy are considerably lower compared to other human activities, such as hydraulic fracturing (fracking) for oil and gas extraction. The focus in geothermal energy projects is typically on harnessing the natural heat from the Earth's interior rather than inducing seismic events. Overall, geothermal energy offers a sustainable and reliable source of clean energy with the potential to contribute to a more sustainable and low-carbon future.

~ 28 ~

BIOMASS ENERGY

Biomass energy is a form of renewable energy derived from organic matter, such as plants, agricultural residues, forestry waste, and dedicated energy crops. It involves the conversion of biomass materials into heat, electricity, or biofuels through various processes. Here are the main types of biomass energy:

Thermal Conversion: Biomass can be burned directly to produce heat or converted into a combustible gas (syngas) through processes like combustion or gasification. The heat generated can be used for heating buildings, industrial processes, or for generating steam to drive turbines for electricity production.

Biochemical Conversion: Biomass can undergo biochemical processes, such as anaerobic digestion or fermentation, to produce biogas or biofuels. Anaerobic digestion involves the breakdown of organic matter by bacteria in the absence of oxygen, resulting in the production of biogas, primarily composed of methane and carbon dioxide. Biofuels, such as ethanol and biodiesel, can be produced through the fermentation of biomass feedstocks like sugarcane, corn, or vegetable oils.

Cogeneration: Biomass energy can be used in combined heat and power (CHP) systems, also known as cogeneration. In these systems, biomass is used to generate both heat and electricity simultaneously, maximizing the energy efficiency of the biomass resource.

Biomass energy is considered renewable because the organic matter used for its production can be replenished through sustainable practices. It has several advantages:

Carbon Neutrality: Biomass energy is considered carbon-neutral because the carbon dioxide emitted during biomass combustion or decomposition is part of the natural carbon cycle. As plants grow, they absorb carbon dioxide from the atmosphere through photosynthesis, offsetting the carbon emissions released when the biomass is used for energy.

Waste Management: Biomass energy can utilize agricultural residues, forestry waste, and other organic materials that would otherwise be left to decompose or be discarded as waste. By converting these materials into energy, biomass can contribute to waste reduction and provide an additional revenue stream for industries and communities.

Local Energy Production: Biomass energy production can be decentralized, allowing for local production and utilization of energy resources. This can enhance energy security, reduce reliance on fossil fuels, and promote economic development in rural areas by creating local jobs and supporting local supply chains.

Flexibility: Biomass energy can be used in various applications, including heat production, electricity generation, and as a feedstock for biofuels. It can be integrated into existing energy infrastructure, providing flexibility in meeting energy demands.

However, biomass energy also has some challenges and considerations, such as the need for sustainable biomass sourcing to prevent deforestation or agricultural conflicts, the potential for air pollutant emissions during combustion, and the competition for land and resources between biomass production and food production.

Arguments over biomass energy often revolve around its benefits, drawbacks, and considerations. Here are some common arguments related to biomass energy:

Renewable Energy Source: Supporters of biomass energy argue that it is a renewable energy source, as it utilizes organic matter derived from plants, crops, agricultural residues, or forest biomass. They highlight the potential of biomass energy to reduce reliance on fossil fuels and contribute to a more sustainable energy mix.

Carbon Neutrality and Climate Change Mitigation: Advocates for biomass energy claim that it can be carbon-neutral or even carbon-negative when sustainably managed. They argue that the carbon emitted during biomass combustion is part of the natural carbon cycle, as the plants absorb carbon dioxide during growth. They see biomass energy as a way to mitigate climate change by reducing greenhouse gas emissions compared to fossil fuel-based energy sources.

Waste Management and Circular Economy: Supporters emphasize the potential for biomass energy to address waste management challenges. They argue that biomass energy can utilize agricultural residues, forestry waste, or organic waste streams, reducing the need for landfill disposal and contributing to a circular economy by converting organic waste into usable energy.

Local Economic Development and Job Creation: Advocates assert that biomass energy projects can stimulate local economies and create job opportunities. They argue that biomass energy production, such as bioenergy plants or pellet production facilities, can generate employment in rural areas, support local supply chains, and contribute to regional economic development.

Energy Independence and Security: Arguments in favor of biomass energy often center around energy independence. Supporters argue that harnessing local biomass resources reduces dependence on imported fossil fuels, enhancing energy security and resilience. They highlight the potential for sustainable biomass energy production to provide a stable and reliable energy supply.

Land Use and Environmental Concerns: Critics of biomass energy raise concerns about land use and potential environmental impacts. They argue that large-scale biomass production may lead to land conversion, deforestation, or competition with food crops, potentially exacerbating land degradation or biodiversity loss. Critics emphasize the importance of sustainable sourcing and proper land management practices to avoid negative environmental consequences.

Air Quality and Emissions: Discussions surrounding biomass energy may touch upon air quality considerations. Critics argue that biomass combustion can release particulate matter, nitrogen oxides, and other air pollutants that may have adverse effects on human health and local air quality. They call for strict emission control measures, efficient combustion technologies, and proper monitoring to mitigate these concerns.

Lifecycle Analysis and Sustainability: Arguments over biomass energy often involve discussions about lifecycle analysis and sustainability assessments. Critics argue that the overall sustainability of biomass energy depends on factors such as feedstock sourcing, transportation, land use practices, and emissions associated with the entire biomass supply chain. They emphasize the importance of comprehensive assessments to ensure the sustainability of biomass energy projects.

Technological Advancements and Innovation: Supporters of biomass energy argue that ongoing technological advancements and innovation can improve efficiency, reduce emissions, and expand the range of biomass feedstocks. They highlight the potential for research and development to address the challenges associated with biomass energy production and optimize its environmental and economic performance.

It's important to note that specific arguments can vary depending on factors such as regional contexts, biomass sources, regulatory frameworks, and stakeholder perspectives. Engaging in informed discussions, considering diverse viewpoints, and conducting comprehensive assessments are crucial for understanding the benefits and challenges of biomass energy and making well-informed decisions.

Overall, biomass energy can play a role in diversifying

energy sources, reducing greenhouse gas emissions, and promoting sustainable development when produced and utilized in an environmentally and socially responsible manner.

Producing biomass energy involves several key steps and considerations. Here are the main aspects involved in the production of biomass energy:

Feedstock Selection: Biomass energy can be derived from various organic materials, known as biomass feedstocks. Common feedstocks include agricultural residues (such as crop residues and animal manure), dedicated energy crops (such as switchgrass or miscanthus), forestry residues (such as wood chips or sawdust), and organic waste (such as food waste or municipal solid waste). The selection of the appropriate feedstock depends on factors such as availability, cost, sustainability, and local regulations.

Feedstock Collection and Handling: Once the feedstock is identified, collection and handling processes are carried out. This involves gathering, sorting, and transporting the biomass feedstock to the processing facility. Proper collection and handling techniques ensure the quality and efficiency of the biomass energy production process.

Biomass Conversion: Biomass conversion refers to the process of converting the biomass feedstock into a usable form of energy. There are several conversion technologies available, including:

Thermochemical Conversion: This includes processes such as combustion, gasification, and pyrolysis, which use heat to convert biomass into a gaseous fuel (syngas), liquid fuel (bio-oil), or solid fuel (charcoal).

Biochemical Conversion: This includes processes such as anaerobic digestion and fermentation, which use microorganisms to break down biomass and produce biogas (methane and carbon dioxide) or liquid biofuels (such as ethanol or biodiesel).

Mechanical/Physical Conversion: This includes processes such as pelletization or briquetting, which compress biomass into denser forms for easier handling and transportation.

The choice of biomass conversion technology depends on factors such as the characteristics of the feedstock, desired energy output, efficiency, and environmental considerations.

Energy Production and Utilization: Once the biomass feedstock is converted into a usable form of energy, it can be utilized for various purposes. Biomass energy can be used for heat generation, electricity production, or as a transportation fuel. Biomass can be burned directly in boilers or furnaces to produce heat or steam, which can be used for industrial processes or heating purposes. Biomass can also be used in power plants to generate electricity through steam turbines. Biomass-derived liquid fuels can be used as transportation fuels, either directly or blended with conventional fossil fuels.

Emissions Control and Environmental Considerations: Biomass energy production should be carried out in a manner that minimizes environmental impacts. Proper emissions control measures, such as the use of pollution control technologies, are important to reduce air pollutants and greenhouse gas emissions. Additionally, sustainable sourcing of biomass feedstock, consideration of land use impacts, and protection of biodiversity are crucial to ensure the long-term environmental sustainability of biomass energy production.

Regulatory Compliance and Certification: Biomass energy production is subject to various regulations and standards to ensure environmental sustainability, quality control, and safety. Compliance with these regulations, such as emissions limits or waste management requirements, is essential. Certification programs, such as sustainability certifications for biomass feedstock, can also provide assurance regarding the sustainable sourcing and production of biomass energy.

Research and Development: Continued research and development efforts are important for improving biomass conversion technologies, increasing efficiency, reducing costs, and exploring new feedstocks. Innovation in biomass energy production can help overcome technical challenges, enhance environmental performance, and make biomass energy more competitive with other energy sources.

Producing biomass energy requires expertise in various fields, including agriculture, engineering, chemistry, and environmental sciences. Collaboration among stakeholders, including biomass suppliers, energy producers, researchers, and policymakers, is crucial for the successful production and utilization of biomass energy.

Biomass energy offers several benefits as a renewable energy source. Here are some of the key advantages of biomass energy:

Renewable and Sustainable: Biomass energy is derived from organic materials, such as agricultural residues, dedicated energy crops, forestry residues, and organic waste. These biomass feedstocks can be replenished through sustainable practices, making biomass energy a renewable energy source. Biomass can be continually grown and harvested, providing a consistent and reliable energy supply.

Reduced Greenhouse Gas Emissions: Biomass energy has the potential to significantly reduce greenhouse gas emissions compared to fossil fuel-based energy sources. While the combustion of biomass releases carbon dioxide (CO_2), the plants used for biomass growth absorb CO_2 during their lifetime, creating a carbon cycle that is considered carbon neutral. By displacing fossil fuels, biomass energy helps reduce net CO_2 emissions and mitigates climate change.

Waste Management and Recycling: Biomass energy provides an opportunity to utilize organic waste materials that would otherwise contribute to landfill waste or emit methane, a potent greenhouse gas. By converting organic waste into energy, biomass energy helps address waste management challenges while providing a renewable energy source.

Local Economic Development: Biomass energy projects can contribute to local economic development by creating job opportunities in feedstock cultivation, collection, and processing. Local communities can benefit from increased employment, income generation, and business opportunities associated with biomass energy production. Biomass energy projects also support local agriculture and forestry sectors by providing a market for feedstocks.

Energy Security and Independence: Biomass energy can enhance energy security by diversifying energy sources and reducing dependence on imported fossil fuels. By utilizing locally available biomass feedstocks, countries can reduce their reliance on external energy sources and promote energy independence.

Baseload and Flexible Power Generation: Biomass power plants can provide baseload electricity generation, meaning they can operate continuously and provide a consistent supply of electricity. Biomass facilities can also be designed to provide flexible power generation, allowing for load following or peak demand support. This flexibility makes biomass energy a valuable asset for grid stability and integration with intermittent renewable energy sources, such as wind and solar.

Co-Generation and Heat Production: Biomass energy systems can be designed for combined heat and power (CHP) generation. CHP facilities simultaneously produce electricity and useful heat, maximizing the efficiency of energy conversion and reducing overall energy waste. Biomass-based heating systems can provide heat for district heating, industrial processes, or residential heating, reducing the need for fossil fuel-based heating systems.

Utilization of Marginal and Underutilized Lands: Biomass feedstocks can be grown on marginal or underutilized lands that are not suitable for food crops. By utilizing these lands for energy crop cultivation, biomass energy production can help optimize land use and contribute to the reclamation of degraded lands.

Grid Stability and Flexibility: Biomass power plants can provide grid stability and support the integration of variable renewable energy sources. Biomass facilities can respond quickly to changes in demand and supply, providing grid stability services such as frequency regulation and grid balancing.

Technological Maturity and Infrastructure: Biomass energy technologies, such as combustion, gasification, and anaerobic digestion, are well-established and have a mature infrastructure. This existing infrastructure makes biomass energy a readily available and scalable option for energy production.

It's important to note that the sustainable sourcing of biomass feedstocks and proper management of the environmental impacts associated with biomass cultivation and processing are crucial to ensuring the overall sustainability and environmental benefits of biomass energy production.

While biomass energy has several benefits as a renewable energy source, there are also some downsides to its utilization. Here are a few potential downsides of biomass energy:

Carbon emissions: While biomass energy is considered renewable, the combustion or decomposition of biomass releases carbon dioxide (CO_2) into the atmosphere. Depending on the source and the efficiency of the conversion process, biomass energy can still contribute to greenhouse gas emissions. In some cases, biomass energy may release more CO_2 than the fossil fuels it is intended to replace, especially if the biomass is not sustainably harvested or managed.

Land and water use: Biomass energy production can require significant land and water resources. Growing crops for biomass, such as corn or sugarcane, may compete with food crops or natural habitats, leading to land-use conflicts and potential deforestation. Additionally, biomass energy production can be water-intensive, particularly in areas already experiencing water scarcity.

Air pollution and health impacts: The combustion of biomass, particularly in traditional or inefficient stoves and boilers, can release pollutants into the air. These pollutants, including particulate matter, nitrogen oxides (NOx), sulfur dioxide (SO_2), and volatile organic compounds (VOCs), can contribute to air pollution and have negative health effects, especially in areas with poor ventilation or high exposure to emissions.

Supply and logistics challenges: Biomass energy requires a consistent and reliable supply of biomass feedstock. However, the availability and quality of biomass resources can vary, depending on factors such as seasonal changes, weather conditions, and regional biomass availability. The logistics of sourcing, storing, and transporting biomass can be complex and may add to the overall cost and feasibility of biomass energy projects.

Potential for unsustainable practices: The production and harvesting of biomass feedstock can have sustainability implications if not managed properly. Unsustainable practices, such as clear-cutting forests or over-harvesting biomass, can lead to ecosystem degradation, loss of biodiversity, and soil erosion. Ensuring the use of sustainable biomass sources and employing responsible land management practices is essential to mitigate these risks.

Technological and efficiency limitations: Biomass energy conversion technologies, such as combustion or anaerobic digestion, may have lower efficiency compared to other renewable energy sources. The energy output per unit of biomass can be relatively low, leading to lower energy conversion efficiencies and potentially higher costs of energy production. Research and development efforts focus on improving the efficiency and effectiveness of biomass energy technologies.

It is important to carefully consider these downsides and address them through sustainable biomass sourcing, advanced conversion technologies, and appropriate emissions controls to ensure that biomass energy is produced and utilized in an environmentally responsible and socially beneficial manner.

It's important to note that biomass energy is generally considered to be a relatively safe and low-risk form of renewable energy. However, like any energy production or industrial process, there is always a potential for accidents or incidents to occur. Here are a few possible examples:

Combustion-related Accidents: Biomass energy is often generated through the combustion of organic materials, such as wood, agricultural residues, or dedicated energy crops. Accidents could potentially occur if there are issues with the combustion process, such as a fire or explosion, which could be a risk in biomass power plants or heating systems.

Supply Chain Accidents: Biomass fuel production and transportation involve various steps, including harvesting, processing, and transportation of feedstock. Accidents like machinery malfunctions, vehicle accidents, or chemical spills during these activities could occur, potentially leading to environmental damage or injury.

Occupational Hazards: Workers involved in the biomass energy sector may face occupational hazards similar to those in other industries, such as mechanical injuries, exposure to chemicals, or falls from height. Proper safety protocols and regulations are necessary to mitigate these risks.

Air Quality Concerns: Biomass combustion can release pollutants into the air, such as particulate matter, nitrogen oxides, and volatile organic compounds. Adequate emission controls and monitoring are essential to minimize the impact on air quality and human health.

It is worth noting that the design, operation, and regulatory frameworks surrounding biomass energy systems are aimed at mitigating and preventing accidents. Governments and regulatory bodies typically have safety regulations and guidelines in place to ensure the safe operation of biomass energy facilities and minimize associated risks.

While accidents are possible in any industry, including biomass energy, adherence to safety protocols, regular maintenance, and proper oversight can help mitigate the risks and ensure the safe and sustainable production of biomass energy.

One could argue that one of the main ingredients in the Oklahoma City Bombing came from biomass energy. According to the FBI, Famous Cases and Criminals, Timothy McVeigh parked a rented Ryder truck in front of the Alfred P. Murrah Federal Building in downtown Oklahoma City, on April 19, 1995. Inside the vehicle was a powerful bomb made out of a deadly cocktail of agricultural fertilizer, diesel fuel, and other chemicals. At precisely 9:02 a.m., the bomb exploded.

Within moments, the surrounding area looked like a war zone. A third of the building had been reduced to rubble, with many floors flattened like pancakes. Dozens of cars were incinerated, and more than 300 nearby buildings were damaged or destroyed. The human toll was still more devastating: 168 souls lost, including 19 children, with several hundred more injured.

It was the worst act of homegrown terrorism in the nation's history.

NUCLEAR POWER

Nuclear power is a form of energy generated through nuclear reactions, specifically through a process called nuclear fission. It involves the splitting of atomic nuclei, typically of uranium or plutonium isotopes, in a controlled manner to release a large amount of energy. Here's how nuclear power works:

Nuclear Reactor: Nuclear power plants contain a nuclear reactor where nuclear fission takes place. The reactor consists of fuel rods containing enriched uranium or plutonium pellets. These fuel rods are arranged in a way that allows the controlled chain reaction of nuclear fission.

Nuclear Fission: During nuclear fission, a neutron is fired at an unstable atomic nucleus, causing it to split into two smaller nuclei. This process releases a significant amount of energy in the form of heat and also generates additional neutrons, which can then cause further fission reactions.

Heat Generation: The energy released during nuclear fission is primarily in the form of heat. This heat is used to produce steam by heating a coolant, such as water, which flows through the reactor core. The steam is then used to drive a turbine.

Electricity Generation: The rotating turbine is connected to a generator, which converts the mechanical energy into electrical energy. The generated electricity is then distributed through a power grid to supply homes, businesses, and industries.

Arguments over nuclear power often revolve around its benefits, drawbacks, and considerations. Here are some common arguments related to nuclear power:

Low Greenhouse Gas Emissions: Supporters of nuclear power emphasize its ability to generate electricity with low greenhouse gas emissions. They argue that nuclear power plants produce minimal carbon dioxide during operation, making it an effective tool for mitigating climate change and reducing reliance on fossil fuels.

Baseload Power Generation: Advocates for nuclear power highlight its capacity for baseload power generation. They argue that nuclear power plants can provide a stable and continuous supply of electricity, contributing to grid stability and meeting high energy demands consistently.

Energy Independence and Security: Arguments in favor of nuclear power often center around energy independence. Supporters argue that domestic nuclear energy production reduces dependence on imported fossil fuels, enhancing energy security and resilience. They highlight the potential for nuclear power to provide a stable and predictable energy supply.

High Energy Density: Supporters emphasize the high energy density of nuclear fuel compared to other energy sources. They argue that a small amount of nuclear fuel can generate a significant amount of electricity, making nuclear power an efficient and space-saving option for meeting energy needs.

Technological Advancements and Innovation: Supporters of nuclear power argue that ongoing technological advancements and innovation can improve safety, reduce waste, and optimize performance. They highlight the potential for advanced reactor designs, such as small modular reactors or Generation IV reactors, to address concerns associated with older reactor technologies.

Job Creation and Economic Benefits: Advocates for nuclear power claim that it can stimulate economic growth and create job opportunities. They argue that nuclear power projects require a skilled workforce and can support employment in various sectors, including construction, operations, and maintenance. They also emphasize the potential for local economic development in communities hosting nuclear power facilities.

Radioactive Waste Management: Critics of nuclear power raise concerns about the long-term management of radioactive waste. They argue that the disposal of high-level nuclear waste poses challenges in terms of safety, security, and environmental impact. Critics emphasize the need for robust waste management strategies and the development of permanent disposal solutions.

Safety and Accidents: Arguments over nuclear power often involve discussions about safety and the potential for accidents. Critics highlight major accidents such as Chernobyl and Fukushima as evidence of the risks associated with nuclear power. They express concerns about the potential for catastrophic accidents, radiation exposure, and the long-term health impacts on nearby communities.

Nuclear Proliferation and Security Risks: Critics may raise concerns about the potential link between nuclear power and nuclear weapons proliferation.

They argue that the technologies and materials used

in nuclear power can pose security risks if not properly controlled and monitored. Critics emphasize the need for stringent international non-proliferation measures and safeguards.

It's important to note that specific arguments can vary depending on factors such as regional contexts, regulatory frameworks, public perception, and stakeholder perspectives. Engaging in informed discussions, considering diverse viewpoints, and conducting comprehensive assessments are crucial for understanding the benefits and challenges of nuclear power and making well-informed decisions.

To establish nuclear power as an energy source, several key factors need to be considered and addressed. Here are the main aspects involved in purposeful nuclear power implementation:

Site Selection and Planning: Identifying suitable sites for nuclear power plants is crucial. Factors such as geological stability, proximity to water sources for cooling, access to transmission infrastructure, and consideration of potential environmental and social impacts must be evaluated. Comprehensive site assessments and feasibility studies are conducted to ensure the suitability and safety of the chosen location.

Regulatory Framework: Establishing a robust regulatory framework is essential to govern the safe and secure operation of nuclear power plants. This includes licensing, inspection, and enforcement processes to ensure compliance with safety standards and regulations. Regulatory bodies play a vital role in overseeing the entire lifecycle of nuclear power plants, from construction and operation to decommissioning and waste management.

Plant Design and Construction: Nuclear power plants require the design and construction of complex infrastructure. This involves engaging expert nuclear engineers, architects, and construction firms to develop and implement designs that adhere to stringent safety standards. The construction process involves rigorous quality control measures, adherence to safety protocols, and coordination with various stakeholders.

Fuel Supply and Management: Establishing a reliable fuel supply chain is crucial for nuclear power plants. This involves securing a sufficient and stable supply of enriched uranium or other nuclear fuel, often through long-term contracts with fuel suppliers. The management of fuel assemblies, including storage, handling, and transport, requires adherence to strict safety protocols and regulatory guidelines.

Safety and Security Measures: Ensuring the safety and security of nuclear power plants is of paramount importance. Comprehensive safety measures, including redundant safety systems, emergency response plans, and rigorous training programs for plant operators, are implemented to prevent accidents and mitigate potential risks. Security measures, including physical protection and safeguards against unauthorized access and nuclear proliferation, are also vital.

Waste Management: Nuclear power generates radioactive waste that must be managed safely and responsibly. Developing and implementing effective waste management strategies, including the handling, storage, and disposal of radioactive materials, is crucial. This may involve the construction of specialized waste storage facilities and adherence to strict regulations for waste transportation and disposal.

Stakeholder Engagement: Engaging with various stakeholders, including local communities, environmental groups, and government bodies, is essential for the acceptance and successful implementation of nuclear power projects. Transparent communication, public consultations, and addressing concerns about safety, environmental impacts, and waste management help build trust and foster support for nuclear power as an energy source.

Training and Education: Building a skilled workforce is vital for the safe and efficient operation of nuclear power plants. Training programs and educational initiatives are necessary to develop a competent workforce of nuclear engineers, operators, technicians, and safety personnel. Collaboration with educational institutions and industry partnerships can help establish robust training programs and knowledge-sharing platforms.

Research and Development: Continuous research and development efforts are crucial to improve nuclear power technologies, enhance safety systems, increase fuel efficiency, and explore advanced concepts, such as advanced reactor designs and nuclear fusion. Government support, industry collaboration, and investment in research facilities are key to driving innovation in the nuclear power sector.

International Cooperation: Nuclear power often involves international cooperation, including the exchange of knowledge, expertise, and best practices. Collaboration among countries in areas such as nuclear safety standards, waste management, and non-proliferation measures helps foster a global nuclear energy community and ensures a harmonized approach to nuclear power implementation.

Implementing nuclear power as an energy source requires significant upfront investment, long-term planning, and strict adherence to safety and regulatory standards. Cooperation among governments, industry stakeholders, and the public is essential for the successful purposeful use of nuclear power to meet energy needs while addressing safety, security, and environmental concerns.

The use of nuclear power as an energy source offers several advantages. Here are some of the key advantages of nuclear power:

Large-Scale Power Generation: Nuclear power plants can generate a significant amount of electricity from a single facility. They have high power density, meaning they can produce large amounts of electricity from a relatively small amount of fuel. This makes nuclear power well-suited for meeting the electricity demands of densely populated areas and industries.

Low Greenhouse Gas Emissions: Nuclear power generation produces very low greenhouse gas emissions, particularly in terms of carbon dioxide (CO_2). Unlike fossil fuel-based power plants, nuclear power plants do not release CO_2 or other air pollutants during operation. This characteristic helps mitigate climate change and reduce the environmental impact of electricity generation.

Baseload Power: Nuclear power plants provide a stable and consistent supply of electricity, making them ideal for baseload power generation. They can operate continuously, supplying a constant amount of electricity to the grid, regardless of weather conditions or fluctuations in energy demand. Nuclear power complements intermittent renewable energy sources, such as wind and solar, by providing a reliable and predictable source of electricity.

Energy Security and Independence: Nuclear power reduces dependence on imported fossil fuels, enhancing energy security and reducing vulnerability to price fluctuations and supply disruptions. Countries with nuclear power capabilities can rely on their own energy resources, reducing their reliance on external sources and enhancing energy independence.

Fuel Efficiency: Nuclear power has a high energy density, meaning a small amount of nuclear fuel can produce a significant amount of energy. Uranium, the most commonly used fuel in nuclear power plants, has a much higher energy content per unit mass compared to fossil fuels. This fuel efficiency reduces the overall fuel consumption and cost of electricity generation.

Stable Fuel Prices: The price of nuclear fuel, such as uranium, is relatively stable compared to the volatility of fossil fuel prices. While the upfront costs of building nuclear power plants can be high, the stability of fuel prices can provide long-term price predictability and help mitigate the impact of fuel price fluctuations on electricity costs.

Job Creation and Economic Impact: The nuclear power industry creates employment opportunities in various sectors, including plant construction, operations, maintenance, and research. Nuclear power plants require a skilled workforce, contributing to local job creation and economic growth. Additionally, the nuclear industry contributes to the development of related industries, such as nuclear engineering, uranium mining, and the manufacturing of nuclear equipment.

Advanced Safety Measures: Modern nuclear power plants incorporate advanced safety features and stringent regulatory standards to ensure the safe operation of the facilities. Safety systems, including multiple layers of containment and emergency response plans, are designed to prevent accidents and protect workers and the public from potential radiation hazards. Lessons learned from past incidents have led to significant improvements in safety practices and designs.

Small Land Footprint: Nuclear power plants have a relatively small land footprint compared to other energy sources with similar power generation capacities. The land required for a nuclear power plant is primarily for the plant infrastructure and does not involve extensive mining or drilling operations. This compactness can be advantageous in areas with limited available land.

Technological Innovation and Research: The development and operation of nuclear power plants drive technological innovation and scientific research. Advances in nuclear science, engineering, and safety practices benefit other industries and contribute to scientific knowledge. Additionally, research efforts in nuclear energy focus on improving reactor designs, enhancing fuel efficiency, and exploring advanced concepts, such as fusion energy.

Despite the advantages of nuclear power, it's important to note that there are concerns related to nuclear waste management, potential accidents, and the proliferation of nuclear weapons. Proper waste disposal, strict regulatory oversight, and ongoing research are essential to address these challenges and ensure the safe and sustainable use of nuclear power.

While nuclear power has certain advantages as an energy source, there are also several downsides and concerns associated with its use. Here are some of the key downsides of using nuclear power:

Radioactive waste: Nuclear power generates radioactive waste that remains hazardous for thousands of years. Proper disposal and long-term management of this waste is a significant challenge. While there are storage facilities for nuclear waste, such as underground repositories, concerns about leakage, accidents, and long-term containment still exist.

Risk of accidents: Nuclear power plants carry the risk of accidents, which can have severe consequences for both human safety and the environment. The most notable example is the Chernobyl disaster in 1986 and the Fukushima disaster in 2011. Although modern reactor designs have improved safety features, accidents can still occur due to human error, equipment failures, or natural disasters.

High initial cost and long construction times: Nuclear power plants require substantial upfront investment and can take many years to construct. The cost of building and maintaining nuclear power plants is generally higher compared to other energy sources. Delays in construction or cost overruns can further increase the financial burden.

Limited fuel supply: Nuclear power relies on uranium or plutonium as fuel, which are finite resources. While there are ample supplies currently available, the long-term sustainability of nuclear power depends on the availability and accessibility of these fuel sources. Additionally, the extraction and processing of nuclear fuel can have environmental impacts.

Proliferation and security risks: The use of nuclear technology for power generation raises concerns about nuclear proliferation and the potential for diversion of nuclear materials for weapons production. The security of nuclear facilities, transportation of radioactive materials, and the prevention of unauthorized access or theft of nuclear materials are ongoing challenges.

Public perception and social acceptance: Nuclear power is a contentious issue, and public perception varies. Concerns about safety, waste management, and the potential for accidents can lead to opposition and limited social acceptance of nuclear power projects. This can affect the feasibility and support for nuclear energy initiatives.

Decommissioning challenges: When nuclear power plants reach the end of their operational life, decommissioning and dismantling them can be a complex and costly process. Proper decommissioning requires safe handling and disposal of radioactive materials and the restoration of the site to minimize environmental impacts.

It is important to recognize and address these downsides and concerns associated with nuclear power through rigorous safety regulations, improved waste management practices, ongoing research and development for advanced reactor designs, and transparent communication with the public. The decision to use nuclear power as an energy source requires careful consideration of the associated risks, benefits, and long-term implications.

I wouldn't want a nuclear plant in my backyard, village, town, city, or county...

One of the most significant nuclear power plant disasters in history is the Chernobyl disaster, which occurred on April 26, 1986, in the Soviet Union (now Ukraine). It remains one of the most catastrophic nuclear accidents to date.

The disaster resulted from a combination of design flaws and operator errors during a safety test at the Chernobyl Nuclear Power Plant's Reactor 4. The test aimed to simulate a power outage and measure the effectiveness of backup systems. However, a series of unforeseen events, including a flawed reactor design and poor operational decisions, led to a runaway reaction, causing a massive steam explosion and subsequent fire.

The explosion released a large amount of radioactive material into the atmosphere, with the fallout spreading over a wide area. The immediate impact was the loss of two plant workers' lives due to the explosion, but the long-term consequences were far more significant. The radioactive cloud contaminated large parts of Ukraine, Belarus, and Russia, and even reached other parts of Europe.

The Chernobyl disaster led to the evacuation and resettlement of hundreds of thousands of people from the affected areas, known as the Exclusion Zone. The release of radioactive materials caused acute radiation sickness in workers and emergency responders, resulting in additional deaths and long-term health effects. The disaster also led to an increased incidence of certain types of cancers and birth defects in the affected populations.

The environmental impact was substantial, with contaminated forests and agricultural lands, as well as contamination of water bodies. The long-term effects on ecosystems and wildlife are still being studied and monitored.

The Chernobyl disaster had a profound impact on nuclear safety regulations and practices worldwide. It highlighted the need for robust safety measures, proper training, and effective communication during emergencies. It also underscored the importance of transparent reporting and international cooperation in dealing with nuclear accidents.

Since Chernobyl, significant improvements in nuclear reactor design, safety protocols, and emergency preparedness have been implemented to reduce the risk of similar accidents. However, the Chernobyl disaster stands as a stark reminder of the potential dangers associated with nuclear power and the importance of ongoing vigilance and adherence to stringent safety standards.

How about Japan? Japan has experienced several weather-related disasters that have impacted nuclear plants in the past. One notable event was the Fukushima Daiichi nuclear disaster in March 2011, triggered by a massive earthquake and subsequent tsunami. The disaster resulted in a severe nuclear accident at the Fukushima Daiichi Nuclear Power Plant, causing the release of radioactive materials and leading to the evacuation of nearby residents.

The earthquake, known as the Great East Japan Earthquake, was one of the most powerful recorded in Japan's history. It generated a tsunami that inundated the Fukushima plant, causing multiple meltdowns, hydrogen explosions, and the release of radioactive contaminants into the environment. The accident prompted a reassessment of nuclear safety measures and led to a significant shift in Japan's energy policy.

Since the Fukushima disaster, Japan has implemented stricter safety regulations and measures for nuclear power plants. The government has also conducted extensive inspections and stress tests to assess the safety and resilience of existing nuclear facilities. Efforts have been made to enhance the resilience of nuclear plants against natural disasters, including reinforcing infrastructure and constructing higher seawalls to protect against tsunamis.

However, it's important to note that no energy infrastructure is completely immune to extreme weather events. Severe weather events, such as typhoons, heavy rainfall, or earthquakes, can pose challenges to the operation and safety of nuclear power plants. To mitigate these risks, ongoing monitoring, maintenance, and preparedness are essential. Emergency response plans, evacuation procedures, and robust communication systems are critical to ensure the safety of plant personnel and nearby communities in the event of a weather-related incident.

Overall, the impact of weather disasters on nuclear plants in Japan highlights the importance of implementing stringent safety measures, conducting thorough risk assessments, and continuously improving the resilience of energy infrastructure. It also underlines the need for diversified energy sources and a comprehensive energy strategy that takes into account both safety and environmental considerations.

Is there one in your backyard? The United States has a significant number of nuclear power plants that contribute to its energy production. There are 93 operating commercial nuclear reactors in the country, spread across 28 states. These reactors generate approximately 20% of the nation's total electricity.

It is important to note that the status of nuclear power plants may change over time due to factors such as aging infrastructure, regulatory decisions, or market conditions. It is advisable to consult up-to-date sources or official websites for the current information on nuclear power plants in the United States.

~ 30 ~

ELECTRIC CARS

An electric car, also known as an electric vehicle (EV), is a type of automobile that is powered by electricity instead of traditional internal combustion engines that run on gasoline or diesel. Electric cars use one or more electric motors to propel the vehicle forward. These motors are powered by rechargeable batteries, which store electricity that is used to drive the wheels and provide the necessary power for the car's operation.

Charging an electric car is done by plugging it into an electric power source, such as a charging station or a home outlet. There are different types of charging options available, including slow charging (using a standard household outlet), fast charging (using dedicated charging stations), and rapid charging (using high-power charging stations). The charging time varies depending on the charging method and the capacity of the car's battery.

As technology advances, electric cars continue to gain popularity and market share. Many major automakers now offer electric car models, and there is a growing infrastructure of charging stations in many regions to support their widespread adoption.

Arguments over electric cars often revolve around their benefits, drawbacks, and considerations. Here are some common arguments related to electric cars:

Environmental Benefits: Supporters of electric cars emphasize their potential to reduce greenhouse gas emissions and combat climate change. They argue that electric vehicles produce zero tailpipe emissions, reducing air pollution and dependence on fossil fuels. Electric cars can contribute to improving air quality, especially in urban areas, and help mitigate the environmental impact of transportation.

Energy Efficiency: Advocates for electric cars highlight their energy efficiency compared to internal combustion engine (ICE) vehicles. They argue that electric drivetrains are more efficient in converting energy into vehicle propulsion, resulting in lower energy consumption and reduced dependence on non-renewable energy sources.

Renewable Energy Integration: Supporters of electric cars argue that they can be part of a larger renewable energy ecosystem. They emphasize the potential for electric vehicles to serve as energy storage devices and facilitate the integration of intermittent renewable energy sources into the grid. By charging during times of excess renewable energy generation, electric cars can help balance electricity supply and demand.

Reduced Dependency on Fossil Fuels: Advocates assert that widespread adoption of electric cars can reduce reliance on fossil fuels and enhance energy security. They argue that diversifying the transportation sector with electric vehicles can reduce vulnerability to oil price fluctuations and geopolitical conflicts related to fossil fuel resources.

Cost Savings: Supporters of electric cars claim that, despite higher upfront costs, they offer long-term cost savings. They argue that electric vehicles have lower operating and maintenance costs compared to ICE vehicles due to the lower cost of electricity, fewer moving parts, and simplified maintenance requirements. Additionally, they highlight potential savings from government incentives, reduced fuel costs, and lower emissions-related charges or taxes.

Charging Infrastructure: Critics of electric cars often raise concerns about the availability and accessibility of charging infrastructure. They argue that the current charging network is insufficient, especially for long-distance travel or in areas with limited charging infrastructure. Critics emphasize the need for widespread charging infrastructure deployment to support the mass adoption of electric vehicles.

Range Anxiety: Arguments against electric cars often revolve around range anxiety, which refers to concerns about the limited driving range and the availability of charging stations. Critics argue that electric cars' range limitations can hinder long-distance travel or cause inconvenience if charging infrastructure is not readily available. They assert that expanding charging networks and improving battery technology are necessary to address these concerns.

Battery Production and Recycling: Critics may raise concerns about the environmental impact of battery production and disposal. They argue that the extraction of materials used in electric vehicle batteries, such as lithium and cobalt, can have environmental and social consequences. Critics emphasize the need for responsible mining practices and efficient battery recycling to minimize the environmental footprint of electric cars.

Technological Advancements: Supporters of electric cars argue that ongoing technological advancements in battery technology, charging infrastructure, and vehicle design will address current limitations and concerns. They highlight the potential for improved battery range, faster charging times, and increased availability of charging stations to further enhance the practicality and appeal of electric cars.

It's important to note that specific arguments can vary depending on factors such as regional contexts, charging infrastructure availability, electricity generation sources, and stakeholder perspectives. Engaging in informed discussions, considering diverse viewpoints, and evaluating the overall lifecycle impacts of electric vehicles are crucial for understanding the benefits and challenges of electric cars and making well-informed decisions.

Myth: Electric cars have limited range and are only suitable for short trips.

Fact: Modern electric cars have significantly improved their range capabilities. Many electric vehicles (EVs) can travel over 200 miles (320 kilometers) on a single charge, and some high-end models can exceed 300 miles (480 kilometers). Additionally, the charging infrastructure is expanding, making long-distance travel more feasible.

Myth: Electric cars are slow and lack power.

Fact: Electric motors provide instant torque, resulting in quick acceleration and responsive performance. Some electric cars, especially high-performance models, can outperform many traditional internal combustion engine vehicles in terms of speed and acceleration.

Myth: Electric cars are not environmentally friendly due to the source of electricity generation.

Fact: While it is true that the environmental impact of an electric car depends on the source of electricity, overall, EVs produce lower emissions compared to internal combustion engine vehicles. As renewable energy sources, such as wind and solar, continue to grow, the carbon footprint of electric cars decreases even further.

Myth: Electric cars are too expensive.

Fact: While electric cars can have a higher upfront cost than traditional vehicles, prices have been decreasing in recent years due to advancements in technology and increased production. Moreover, the total cost of ownership for electric cars can be lower over time due to savings on fuel and maintenance costs.

Myth: Charging infrastructure is insufficient and inconvenient.

Fact: The charging infrastructure for electric vehicles is continually expanding. Public charging stations are becoming more common in urban areas, and many businesses, shopping centers, and parking facilities offer charging facilities. Home charging stations are also an option, allowing convenient overnight charging.

Myth: Electric car batteries degrade quickly, resulting in high replacement costs.

Fact: Battery technology has significantly improved, and modern electric car batteries are designed to have a long lifespan. Most manufacturers offer warranties on their batteries for a certain number of years or miles, ensuring their durability and reliability.

Research: Electric car batteries typically consist of several key materials, including:

Lithium: Lithium is a crucial component of electric vehicle (EV) batteries. It is commonly used in the form of lithium-ion batteries due to its high energy density. Lithium resources are found in various countries, including Australia, Chile, China, Argentina, and Zimbabwe. Extracting lithium involves mining and processing lithium-bearing minerals or extracting lithium from underground brine deposits.

Cobalt: Cobalt is used in the cathode of lithium-ion batteries to enhance their stability and performance. The majority of cobalt production comes from the Democratic Republic of Congo (DRC), followed by countries like Russia, Australia, and Canada. There have been concerns about ethical and environmental issues related to cobalt mining, including child labor and environmental degradation.

Nickel: Nickel is another key component of lithium-ion batteries, particularly in high-energy-density cathodes. It helps improve the energy storage capacity of the battery. Nickel production is widespread, with major producers including Indonesia, the Philippines, Russia, Canada, and Australia.

Graphite: Graphite is used in the anode of lithium-ion batteries. It helps store and release lithium ions during charging and discharging cycles. The main graphite producers include China, Brazil, Canada, and India. Synthetic graphite is often used in EV batteries due to its higher purity and better performance.

Manganese: Manganese is sometimes used in lithium-ion battery cathodes, along with nickel and cobalt. It contributes to stability and helps balance the performance and cost of the battery. Manganese is primarily produced in countries like South Africa, Australia, China, and Gabon.

Other Materials: Electric vehicle batteries may also contain small amounts of other materials such as aluminum, copper, electrolytes (typically composed of salts), and various additives to enhance battery performance, safety, and longevity.

It's important to note that the availability and sources of these materials can change over time as new technologies are developed and the demand for electric vehicle batteries increases. Efforts are being made to improve the sustainability and ethical sourcing of these materials, ensuring responsible mining practices, and promoting recycling and reuse of battery components to minimize environmental impact.

Furthermore, the development of next-generation batteries, such as solid-state batteries and alternative chemistries, aims to reduce or eliminate the reliance on certain materials like cobalt and increase the energy density and sustainability of electric vehicle batteries.

Before judging electric vehicle batteries, ask yourself about your cell phone battery. Cell phone batteries, specifically lithium-ion (Li-ion) batteries, consist of several key materials. Here's a breakdown of the main components and their sources:

Cathode Materials:

Lithium Cobalt Oxide (LiCoO2): This is a commonly used cathode material in cell phone batteries. The cobalt used in LiCoO2 cathodes mainly comes from countries like the Democratic Republic of Congo (DRC), Russia, and Australia.

Lithium Iron Phosphate (LiFePO4): LiFePO4 cathodes are another type of cathode material used in cell phone batteries. The raw materials for iron and phosphate are widely available globally.

Anode Materials:

Graphite: Graphite is the most commonly used anode material in cell phone batteries. The graphite used in the industry is often sourced from countries such as China, India, Brazil, and Canada.

Electrolyte:

Lithium Hexafluorophosphate (LiPF6): LiPF6 is a common electrolyte salt used in lithium-ion batteries, including those in cell phones. The production and supply of LiPF6 are mainly centered in countries like China, Japan, and South Korea.
Separator:

Polyethylene or Polypropylene: The separator, which keeps the cathode and anode separate, is typically made of polyethylene or polypropylene. These materials are widely produced and available globally.

Current Collectors:

Aluminum and Copper: Aluminum foils are commonly used as the current collector for the cathode, while copper foils are used as the current collector for the anode. These metals are widely produced and sourced from various countries.
Myth: Electric cars are not suitable for cold climates.

Fact: Electric cars perform well in cold climates, although extreme temperatures can affect battery performance to some extent. Manufacturers design EVs with thermal management systems to optimize battery performance and maintain efficiency in various weather conditions.

It's important to note that the specific details and performance of electric cars can vary depending on the make, model, and technology. Keeping up with the latest information and consulting reliable sources is crucial when evaluating electric cars and understanding their capabilities.

Electric cars, also known as electric vehicles (EVs), offer several advantages compared to traditional internal combustion engine vehicles. Here are some of the key advantages of electric cars:

Environmental Benefits: Electric cars produce zero tailpipe emissions, which means they do not release pollutants such as carbon dioxide (CO_2), nitrogen oxides (NOx), and particulate matter. By replacing fossil fuel-powered vehicles with electric cars, we can significantly reduce air pollution and greenhouse gas emissions, helping to mitigate climate change and improve air quality.

Energy Efficiency: Electric cars are more energy-efficient compared to internal combustion engine vehicles. They convert a higher percentage of the energy stored in the battery to power the wheels, whereas traditional cars waste a significant amount of energy as heat. This higher efficiency translates into reduced energy consumption and lower operating costs.

Renewable Energy Integration: Electric cars can be charged using electricity generated from renewable sources such as solar, wind, and hydropower. This allows for the integration of clean, sustainable energy into the transportation sector, reducing dependence on fossil fuels and supporting the transition to a renewable energy future.

Cost Savings: While electric cars may have a higher upfront cost compared to conventional vehicles, they tend to have lower operating costs over their lifetime. Electricity is generally cheaper than gasoline or diesel fuel, resulting in lower fuel costs for electric car owners. Additionally, electric cars have fewer moving parts and require less maintenance, leading to potential long-term cost savings.

Reduced Noise Pollution: Electric cars operate much quieter than internal combustion engine vehicles. Their electric motors produce minimal noise, contributing to quieter and more peaceful urban environments. This can have positive impacts on reducing noise pollution in cities and improving the overall quality of life for residents.

Performance and Instant Torque: Electric motors provide instant torque, delivering quick acceleration and responsive performance. Electric cars often have impressive acceleration capabilities and can provide a smooth and enjoyable driving experience.

Energy Security and Independence: Electric cars offer the potential for reduced dependence on fossil fuel imports. By shifting to electric transportation and utilizing locally generated renewable energy, countries can enhance their energy security and reduce their reliance on foreign oil.

It's important to note that the benefits of electric cars can vary depending on factors such as the electricity generation mix, driving patterns, and charging infrastructure availability. However, as the technology continues to advance and renewable energy becomes more prevalent, the advantages of electric cars are expected to further increase.

However, like any other technology, electric cars also come with their own set of potential risks and considerations. Here are some of the dangers associated with electric cars:

Battery-related hazards: Electric car batteries store

a significant amount of energy, and while they are generally safe, there are potential risks associated with battery malfunction or damage. In rare cases, lithium-ion batteries can experience thermal runaway, leading to overheating, fires, or even explosions. However, extensive safety measures and advanced battery management systems are in place to minimize these risks.

Charging infrastructure risks: Electric cars rely on charging infrastructure for recharging their batteries. Public charging stations, like any electrical infrastructure, may have potential risks such as electrical faults, malfunctions, or even tampering. It is essential to use properly maintained and certified charging stations to minimize these risks.

Electric shock hazards: Electric vehicles operate at high voltages, typically 400 to 800 volts, which can present risks of electric shock in case of contact with live parts. However, electric cars are designed with robust insulation systems, safety mechanisms, and compliance with relevant electrical safety standards to minimize these risks. It is crucial to follow safe practices and avoid tampering with the electrical components of an electric vehicle.

Emergency response considerations: Emergency responders, such as firefighters or paramedics, need to be trained to handle incidents involving electric vehicles. Electric cars have unique characteristics that responders should be aware of, such as high-voltage systems, specialized battery handling procedures, and the risk of electric shock. Proper training and education are essential to ensure effective and safe emergency response.

Environmental concerns: While electric cars contribute to reducing greenhouse gas emissions during their operation, the production and disposal of batteries and other components may have environmental implications. Proper management of battery waste, recycling, and sustainable manufacturing practices are crucial to mitigate these risks and ensure the overall environmental benefits of electric vehicles.

It's important to note that the risks associated with electric cars are generally low compared to the risks associated with conventional internal combustion engine vehicles, such as fuel-related fires or emissions-related health hazards. The automotive industry and regulatory bodies continuously work to enhance the safety standards and address potential risks associated with electric vehicles.

As with any technology, it is important for consumers to stay informed about the latest safety guidelines, follow manufacturer recommendations, and adhere to proper maintenance practices to ensure the safe and responsible use of electric cars.

The current infrastructure for electric cars is continuously improving but still faces some challenges in certain areas. Here are some considerations regarding the existing infrastructure and its support for electric cars:

Charging infrastructure: The availability and accessibility of charging stations are crucial for the widespread adoption of electric cars. While the number of charging stations has been increasing globally, there are still areas with limited charging infrastructure, especially in rural or remote locations. Urban areas and developed regions generally have a more established network of charging stations. However, further expansion is needed to ensure convenient access to charging points, including fast-charging options for longer trips.

Charging speeds: The time it takes to charge an electric car varies depending on the charging station type. Level 1 charging, which uses a standard household outlet, is the slowest, while Level 2 charging (typically available in homes, workplaces, and public charging stations) provides faster charging. Fast-charging stations (DC fast chargers) offer even quicker charging times. The availability and distribution of fast-charging stations need to be expanded to support long-distance travel and reduce charging times for electric car owners.

Grid capacity and power demand: The widespread adoption of electric cars will increase the demand for electricity, which can strain the power grid if not managed properly. Utilities and grid operators need to plan and invest in infrastructure upgrades to accommodate the increased power demand, especially during peak charging periods. Smart grid technologies, load management strategies, and time-of-use pricing can help optimize electricity distribution and balance the power grid.

Home charging infrastructure: Many electric car owners rely on home charging as a primary source of recharging. Ensuring that residential electrical systems can handle the increased demand for charging is essential. Adequate electrical capacity, such as sufficient circuitry and appropriate charging equipment installation, is necessary to support home charging needs.

Future infrastructure developments: Governments, utilities, and private entities are investing in the expansion and improvement of charging infrastructure. Initiatives include the installation of public charging stations, partnerships with businesses to provide charging facilities, and the integration of charging infrastructure with renewable energy sources. These efforts aim to enhance the charging experience and address the current infrastructure gaps.

While the current infrastructure may have limitations, it is important to recognize that it is continuously evolving and expanding. Governments and industry stakeholders are actively working to improve the charging infrastructure to support the growing adoption of electric cars. Additionally, advancements in technology, such as higher-capacity batteries and faster-charging options, are being developed to enhance the convenience and efficiency of electric vehicle charging.

Overall, while challenges exist, the infrastructure to support electric cars is gradually improving, and with ongoing investments and developments, it is expected to better accommodate the increasing demand for electric vehicles in the future.

Here is what you need to know about an electric car's battery and the controversies surrounding the batteries:

Environmental Impact of Battery Production: The production of electric car batteries involves mining and processing raw materials, which can have environmental impacts such as habitat destruction, water pollution, and carbon emissions. Additionally, the extraction of certain materials like cobalt has raised concerns about unethical mining practices and human rights violations in some regions.

Carbon Footprint: While electric vehicles produce zero tailpipe emissions during operation, the carbon footprint of an electric car includes not only its use but also the production and disposal of the battery. The energy-intensive manufacturing processes for batteries, particularly in regions where electricity generation is still reliant on fossil fuels, can contribute to a significant carbon footprint.

Battery Recycling and End-of-Life Disposal: Electric car batteries have a limited lifespan, typically ranging from 8 to 15 years depending on usage. There are concerns about the recycling and proper disposal of used batteries. Establishing efficient recycling processes to recover valuable materials and minimize environmental impact is essential. However, the infrastructure and technology for large-scale battery recycling are still developing.

Resource Availability and Dependence: The global supply of certain battery materials, such as lithium, cobalt, and nickel, can be limited. This raises concerns about the dependence of the electric vehicle industry on a few key materials and the potential for resource shortages or price volatility. Efforts are being made to develop alternative battery chemistries that use fewer or more readily available materials.

Energy Density and Range Anxiety: Electric car batteries have made significant advancements in energy density, allowing for longer driving ranges. However, concerns about limited range, known as "range anxiety," still exist, particularly for long-distance travel or in regions with inadequate charging infrastructure.

Continued innovation in battery technology is needed to improve energy density and charging speed.

It's important to note that the electric vehicle industry is actively addressing these controversies. Automakers and battery manufacturers are working towards reducing the environmental impact of battery production, improving recycling processes, and developing more sustainable battery chemistries. Efforts are also being made to increase the availability of charging infrastructure and develop new battery technologies with improved energy density and reduced reliance on critical materials.

Shortly after announcing that California was banning gasoline cars and transitioning to electric cars by 2035, they experienced rolling blackouts. Rolling blackouts occur when there is an imbalance between electricity supply and demand, leading to temporary power outages. Several factors contributed to the rolling blackouts in California, including:

Heatwaves and extreme weather events: California experienced heatwaves and wildfires, which put a strain on the electricity grid. High temperatures increase the demand for electricity as people rely on air conditioning, and wildfires can damage power infrastructure, leading to power disruptions.

Dependence on renewable energy sources: California has made significant progress in adopting renewable energy sources, such as solar and wind power. However, renewable energy generation can be intermittent and dependent on weather conditions. During times of high demand and low renewable energy production, there may be a shortfall in electricity supply.

Grid infrastructure challenges: The electricity grid infrastructure in California faced challenges in terms of aging infrastructure, transmission bottlenecks, and limited interconnection capacity. These issues can impact the reliable transmission of electricity across the state, especially during periods of high demand.

Natural gas supply constraints: California relies on natural gas power plants for a significant portion of its electricity generation. However, during the rolling blackouts, there were issues with the availability of natural gas due to pipeline limitations and supply constraints, further exacerbating the electricity supply-demand imbalance.

It's worth noting that the transition to electric cars by 2035 is a long-term goal aimed at reducing greenhouse gas emissions and promoting sustainable transportation. The successful implementation of this goal will require a comprehensive approach, including investment in charging infrastructure, grid upgrades, and demand management strategies to ensure a reliable and resilient electricity system.

To address the challenges associated with transitioning to electric vehicles and maintaining a stable electricity grid, planning and coordination between government agencies, utilities, and industry stakeholders are crucial. This includes strategies such as energy storage systems, demand response programs, and grid modernization efforts to support the increased electricity demand from electric vehicles while ensuring grid reliability.

Concerns about government control over electricity usage when mandating electric cars are understandable, but it's important to consider the broader context and the actual implications of such mandates. Here are a few points to consider:

Mandates versus restrictions: When governments set targets or mandates for electric vehicle adoption, they are typically focused on promoting the transition to cleaner and more sustainable transportation. Mandates often involve goals and incentives rather than direct restrictions on electricity usage. The aim is to reduce greenhouse gas emissions, improve air quality, and address climate change concerns.

Consumer choice and market dynamics: Mandates for electric vehicles do not typically involve the government dictating how individuals use electricity on a day-to-day basis. Consumers still have the freedom to choose how and when to charge their vehicles based on their needs and preferences. The market for electric vehicles and associated charging infrastructure is driven by consumer demand and private sector investments.

Grid management and infrastructure development: As electric vehicle adoption increases, grid management becomes a consideration. However, managing the electricity grid to accommodate the changing needs of electric vehicles is a technical challenge, not necessarily a form of control. Grid operators and utilities work to ensure the stability and reliability of the grid while integrating renewable energy sources and managing charging demands.

Collaboration and stakeholder involvement: Government initiatives related to electric vehicles often involve collaboration with various stakeholders, including utilities, charging infrastructure providers, and automotive manufacturers. These collaborations help ensure that policies and strategies are developed through a consultative and inclusive process, taking into account the interests and concerns of all involved parties.

Checks and balances: In democratic societies, government actions and policies are subject to checks and balances through legal frameworks, public scrutiny, and accountability mechanisms. This helps prevent excessive government control and promotes transparency and accountability in decision-making processes.

It's essential for governments to strike a balance between promoting sustainable transportation and respecting individual freedoms and choices. By setting goals and providing incentives for electric vehicle adoption, governments aim to create a more sustainable and environmentally friendly transportation system, without necessarily exerting undue control over electricity usage.

As with any policy or mandate, it's important for individuals to stay informed, engage in public discourse, and participate in the democratic process to shape and influence decisions that affect their lives. I know that I personally have concerns over this situation in the near future.

There is a meme floating around on social media that shows a truck that runs on diesel, that is pulling a generator, which runs on gasoline, charging an electric car – it cracks me up!

~ 31 ~

ENVIRONMENTAL EDUCATION AND AWARENESS

Achieving environmental education and awareness is crucial for promoting sustainable behaviors, empowering individuals, and communities to take action, and fostering a deeper understanding of environmental challenges. Here are some strategies to achieve environmental education and awareness:

Formal education: Incorporate environmental education into school curricula at all levels, from elementary to higher education. Integrate environmental concepts into various subjects and provide hands-on experiences, field trips, and practical learning opportunities.

Non-formal education: Promote environmental education outside traditional academic settings through workshops, seminars, community events, and nature-based programs. Collaborate with environmental organizations, museums, parks, and community centers to provide experiential learning and outreach activities.

Public campaigns and awareness-raising: Conduct public awareness campaigns through various channels such as media, social media, public events, and community forums. Use compelling messages, visuals, and storytelling techniques to engage and inform the public about environmental issues, their impacts, and potential solutions.

Engage with diverse audiences: Tailor environmental education initiatives to address the specific needs and interests of different age groups, communities, and cultural backgrounds. Recognize and incorporate diverse perspectives and values in environmental discussions to foster inclusivity.

Partnerships and collaborations: Collaborate with government agencies, educational institutions, NGOs, businesses, and community organizations to strengthen environmental education initiatives. Pool resources, share expertise, and coordinate efforts to reach wider audiences and maximize impact.

Teacher training and professional development: Provide training programs for teachers and educators to enhance their knowledge and skills in delivering environmental education effectively. Offer professional development opportunities, workshops, and resources that align with current environmental issues and teaching methodologies.

Hands-on learning and citizen science: Encourage participation in citizen science projects and experiential learning activities that allow individuals to contribute to environmental research and monitoring efforts. This fosters a sense of ownership, curiosity, and understanding of environmental issues.

Environmental leadership and youth engagement: Empower youth to become environmental leaders by providing platforms for their ideas, initiatives, and involvement in decision-making processes. Support youth-led organizations, projects, and campaigns focused on environmental sustainability.

Promote behavior change: Link environmental education with action-oriented initiatives that encourage sustainable behaviors. Provide practical tips, guidelines, and resources for individuals and communities to adopt eco-friendly practices in their daily lives.

Continuous learning and lifelong education: Foster a culture of continuous learning and lifelong education by promoting access to environmental information, resources, and opportunities for ongoing engagement. Encourage individuals to stay informed, explore new knowledge, and adapt their behaviors in response to changing environmental issues.

It's important to evaluate the effectiveness of environmental education initiatives and adapt approaches based on feedback and outcomes. By combining these strategies, we can enhance environmental education and awareness, fostering a more informed and environmentally conscious society. But there are challenges to environmental education and awareness. Some of the key challenges include:

Limited resources: Environmental education programs often face constraints in terms of funding, staff, and infrastructure. Insufficient resources can restrict the development and implementation of comprehensive and impactful initiatives.

Curriculum constraints: Education systems may have rigid curricula that prioritize core subjects, leaving limited space for environmental education. Incorporating environmental topics into existing curricula can be challenging, requiring coordination and support from educational authorities.

Lack of teacher training: Many teachers may not have received adequate training in environmental education, making it difficult for them to effectively deliver environmental concepts and engage students. Providing ongoing professional development opportunities for educators is crucial to address this challenge.

Complexity of environmental issues: Environmental challenges are multifaceted and complex, often requiring an interdisciplinary approach. Communicating and teaching these issues in a way that is accessible and engaging for various audiences can be challenging.

Inadequate access to information and resources: Some communities, particularly those in underserved areas, may lack access to up-to-date and reliable environmental information and resources. Bridging this information gap is essential for promoting widespread environmental education and awareness.

Limited integration into formal education systems: While environmental education may exist as a separate subject or module in some schools, its integration into the broader curriculum can be limited. A more holistic approach that incorporates environmental concepts into multiple subjects is needed.

Lack of awareness and prioritization: Environmental issues may not be seen as immediate or pressing concerns by individuals or decision-makers. Raising awareness about the urgency and interconnectedness of environmental challenges is necessary to drive action and support for environmental education initiatives.

Cultural and language barriers: Environmental education should consider cultural diversity and address language barriers to effectively reach and engage diverse populations. Approaches that are sensitive to local cultures, languages, and knowledge systems can help overcome these challenges.

Behavioral change and long-term impact: While environmental education can raise awareness, translating that awareness into meaningful behavior change can be difficult. Shifting attitudes and habits toward more sustainable practices requires ongoing reinforcement, support, and collaboration with other sectors.

Monitoring and evaluation: Assessing the impact of environmental education and awareness initiatives can be challenging. Establishing robust monitoring and evaluation frameworks to measure changes in knowledge, attitudes, and behaviors is essential to understand the effectiveness of these programs and make necessary improvements.

Addressing these challenges requires collaborative efforts from educational institutions, governments, NGOs, communities, and individuals. Adequate investment in resources, teacher training, curriculum development, and community engagement is crucial to overcome these obstacles and foster effective environmental education and awareness.

INTERNATIONAL COOPERATION AND POLICY FRAMEWORKS

International cooperation and policy frameworks play a vital role in addressing global environmental challenges and working towards saving our planet. Here are some key aspects of international cooperation and policy frameworks:

United Nations Framework Convention on Climate Change (UNFCCC): The UNFCCC is an international treaty that provides a framework for global cooperation to combat climate change. It sets the goal of stabilizing greenhouse gas concentrations in the atmosphere to prevent dangerous human interference with the climate system.

Paris Agreement: The Paris Agreement, adopted under the UNFCCC, is a landmark international treaty aimed at limiting global warming to well below 2 degrees Celsius above pre-industrial levels and pursuing efforts to limit the temperature increase to 1.5 degrees Celsius. It establishes a framework for countries to set their own nationally determined contributions (NDCs) and promotes transparency, accountability, and international cooperation in climate action.

Sustainable Development Goals (SDGs): The SDGs, adopted by the United Nations, provide a comprehensive framework for sustainable development, encompassing social, economic, and environmental dimensions. Goal 13 specifically focuses on climate action, emphasizing the need for urgent action to combat climate change and its impacts.

International environmental conventions: Several international conventions address specific environmental issues, such as the Convention on Biological Diversity (CBD), the Convention on International Trade in Endangered Species of Wild Fauna and Flora (CITES), and the Basel Convention on the Control of Transboundary Movements of Hazardous Wastes and Their Disposal. These conventions promote cooperation among nations to protect biodiversity, combat wildlife trafficking, and manage hazardous waste.

Global environmental governance: International organizations, such as the United Nations Environment Program (UNEP) and regional bodies like the European

Union (EU), play a crucial role in coordinating global environmental efforts, providing technical assistance, facilitating negotiations, and monitoring progress towards environmental goals.

Financial mechanisms: International cooperation involves financial mechanisms to support developing countries in their efforts to address environmental challenges. These mechanisms include the Green Climate Fund, which aims to mobilize funding for climate change adaptation and mitigation projects in developing countries.

Technology transfer and capacity building: International cooperation facilitates the transfer of environmentally sound technologies, knowledge, and best practices among countries. Capacity building initiatives help developing countries strengthen their institutional, technical, and human resources to tackle environmental issues effectively.

Cross-border collaboration: Many environmental challenges, such as air and water pollution, biodiversity loss, and climate change, transcend national boundaries. International cooperation enables countries to collaborate on shared environmental issues, establish joint monitoring and management frameworks, and implement cross-border initiatives.

Public-private partnerships: Collaboration between

governments, businesses, and civil society organizations is crucial for effective environmental action. Public-private partnerships promote innovation, resource sharing, and collective action in areas such as renewable energy, sustainable agriculture, and conservation.

Knowledge sharing and science-policy interface: International cooperation facilitates the exchange of scientific research, data, and information to inform policy decisions. Strengthening the science-policy interface helps ensure evidence-based decision-making and the integration of scientific knowledge into policy frameworks.

While international cooperation and policy frameworks provide a foundation for collective action, their effectiveness relies on political commitment, implementation, and ongoing monitoring and evaluation. Continued collaboration, shared responsibilities, and a sense of urgency are necessary to address the pressing environmental challenges facing our planet.

Achieving international cooperation and policy frameworks for saving our planet faces several obstacles. These obstacles can hinder progress and make it challenging to reach consensus and implement effective measures. Here are some key obstacles:

Differing national interests: Nations have diverse

priorities, economic conditions, and political dynamics, which can create challenges in aligning their interests and goals. Disagreements over burden-sharing, responsibilities, and resource allocation can hinder the development of effective international cooperation and policy frameworks.

Political barriers: Political dynamics, power struggles, and changes in leadership can impede international cooperation. Political instability, conflicts, and competing national agendas can disrupt the continuity of efforts and hinder long-term commitments to environmental action.

Economic considerations: Economic interests and the perceived trade-offs between environmental protection and economic growth can pose challenges. Some countries may be hesitant to adopt ambitious environmental policies due to concerns about their economic competitiveness or the potential impacts on specific industries.

Equity and fairness concerns: Developing countries often face capacity limitations, financial constraints, and technology gaps in addressing environmental challenges. Ensuring equity and fairness in international cooperation can be challenging, as countries seek to balance their own development needs with their global responsibilities.

Lack of trust: Building trust among nations is crucial for effective international cooperation. Historical tensions, geopolitical rivalries, and differences in approaches can lead to skepticism and a lack of confidence in joint efforts, hindering collaboration on global environmental issues.

Compliance and enforcement: The effectiveness of international cooperation relies on compliance with agreed-upon commitments and the enforcement of policies. Weak enforcement mechanisms, limited penalties for non-compliance, and the absence of universally binding agreements can undermine the impact of policy frameworks.

Data and information gaps: Adequate and reliable data on environmental issues are essential for informed decision-making and effective policy formulation. However, data gaps, inconsistent methodologies, and limited accessibility to data can hinder efforts to assess the scale of environmental challenges and design appropriate solutions.

Communication and language barriers: Effective communication is crucial for international cooperation. Language barriers, cultural differences, and varying levels of scientific literacy can hinder the understanding and effective exchange of ideas, knowledge, and perspectives.

Lack of public awareness and support: Public support and engagement are essential for effective implementation of environmental policies. However, limited public awareness, misconceptions, and skepticism about environmental issues can undermine the political will and societal pressure needed for ambitious action.

Time constraints and urgency: Addressing global environmental challenges requires urgent and timely action. However, the pace of international negotiations, decision-making processes, and bureaucratic complexities can delay the adoption and implementation of effective policies, compromising their impact.

Overcoming these obstacles requires sustained diplomatic efforts, strengthened international institutions, and enhanced dialogue among nations. Building trust, promoting transparency, providing capacity-building support, and fostering meaningful public participation are essential to foster international cooperation and overcome the challenges to save our planet. We shouldn't rely on our governments to solve the problems; we can start at the lowest level and work our way up.

~ 33 ~

GOVERNING POLICY

In his Inaugural Address, on January 20, 1981, Ronald Reagan said, "In this present crisis, government is not the solution to our problem; government is the problem. From time to time, we've been tempted to believe that society has become too complex to be managed by self-rule, that government by an elite group is superior to government for, by, and of the people. Well, if no one among us is capable of governing himself, then who among us has the capacity to govern someone else? All of us together, in and out of government, must bear the burden. ... demand recognition of the distinction between the powers granted to the Federal Government and those reserved to the States or to the people. All of us need to be reminded that the Federal Government did not create the States; the States created the Federal Government."[9]

Policy decisions in a country often involve multiple levels of government, from the local or municipal level to the regional, state, or provincial level, and ultimately to the federal or central government. Here's an overview of how policy decisions can be formed and implemented at different levels:

Local Government: Local governments, such as city councils or municipal bodies, have jurisdiction over specific geographical areas. They are responsible for local governance and often make policy decisions related to issues that directly affect their communities. These decisions can involve matters like zoning regulations, local infrastructure development, public transportation, waste management, and public health initiatives.

Regional or State/Provincial Government: In countries with a federal or decentralized system, regional or state/provincial governments have authority over larger geographic areas within the country. They have more extensive powers and are responsible for policy decisions that impact their respective regions or states. These decisions may include education policies, healthcare services, transportation infrastructure, economic development strategies, and environmental regulations.

Federal or Central Government: The federal or central government represents the highest level of governance in a country. It typically has jurisdiction over national and international affairs, defense, foreign relations, and overarching policy areas that affect the entire country. Federal governments make policy decisions on issues such as taxation, national security, immigration, trade, healthcare systems, social welfare programs, environmental regulations, and constitutional matters.

Policy decisions are often made through a legislative process involving elected representatives and government officials. This process typically includes:

Proposal and Development: Policy proposals can originate from various sources, including government departments, elected officials, advocacy groups, or public consultations. Relevant stakeholders analyze the issue, conduct research, and develop policy options.

Legislation and Debate: If the policy proposal gains support, it can be introduced as a bill or legislation in the appropriate legislative body. The bill goes through readings, debates, and committee reviews, allowing for amendments and input from different stakeholders.

Voting and Adoption: After the bill has been thoroughly discussed, it is put to a vote. If the majority of the legislators or representatives support the bill, it is adopted as law.

Implementation and Enforcement: Once a policy is enacted, the responsible government agencies and departments develop implementation plans, allocate resources, and enforce compliance with the policy. This may involve creating regulations, monitoring compliance, and providing oversight.

It's important to note that the specific processes and structures for policy decision-making can vary between countries based on their political systems and legal frameworks. Additionally, there may be interactions and coordination between different levels of government to ensure cohesive policies and effective governance across the country.

The complexity of policy decisions, simply starts with "We the People." The power that we give to our governing bodies starts at the local level: Village, Town, City, County, State, and finally Federal. It is our responsibility to continue to voice our demands of the needed changes to save of planet and what steps we want them to take to do so. We must lead by example and realize the impact we can make, because we aren't the only one's living on this planet.

One-billion people live in urban slums. 1.5 billion people live in countries affected by repeated cycles of violence. In the past decade, the number of people affected by natural disasters tripled to 2 billion. Low-income countries have accounted for only 9% of the disaster events but 48% of fatalities in the last 45 years. The burden of disasters, conflict, crime, and violence falls disproportionately on the poor.

Our oceans play an integral role in climate change mitigation, absorbing some 23% of human-caused carbon dioxide emissions and more than 90% of the excess heat created by human-caused greenhouse gases. Climate Change disrupts ocean patterns, and thus fish distribution and migration patterns, with a direct risk to food security of fish-dependent coastal communities.

Life on land will experience more frequent and intense drought, storms, heat waves, rising sea levels, melting glaciers, and warming oceans can directly harm animals, destroy the places they live, and wreak havoc on people's livelihoods and communities.

The unfortunate reality of these issues are incentives for individuals and corporations to actively participate in programs that will make our planet heathier. Humans, especially today, want to see immediate results for their efforts. There is a lack of understanding of long-term efforts and affects. Or there is a lack of compassion for how we will leave this earth for the next generations. We, as humans, must become a more effective caregiver to our planet. Through Global Citizenship Awareness Training, increase cogitative learning to develop patterns of behavior that will ultimately contribute to the reduction of the negative impact and increase positive impact on our planet.

34

BECOMING A GLOBAL CITIZEN

Global Citizenship: An awareness that you are part of the human family, "and going beyond your interests to recognize the needs and challenges in resolving some of the problems that the world is faced with."[4] The UN goes on to define Global Citizenship "... as the concept that one's identity transcends, even as it respects, geographical and national borders, and that our social, political, environmental and economic actions occur in an interconnected world."[5]

An educated person is an informed person. We must continue to grow as an informed society. Global citizenship education is of significant importance in today's interconnected and interdependent world. Global citizen education refers to the process of providing individuals with the knowledge, skills, and attitudes necessary to understand and engage with global issues, promote social justice, and contribute to a more sustainable and inclusive world. It aims to foster a sense of global citizenship, where individuals recognize their interconnectedness with others, both locally and globally, and take responsibility for addressing global challenges.

Here are some key aspects of global citizen education:

Global Awareness: Global citizen education promotes understanding of global issues such as poverty, inequality, climate change, human rights, peace, and sustainable development. It encourages individuals to recognize the interconnected nature of these issues and the impact they have on people and the planet.

Intercultural Competence: Global citizen education emphasizes the development of intercultural skills and sensitivity, enabling individuals to communicate, collaborate, and build relationships with people from diverse cultures, backgrounds, and perspectives. It fosters respect, empathy, and appreciation for cultural diversity.

Critical Thinking: Global citizen education encourages individuals to think critically and analytically about complex global issues. It promotes the ability to evaluate information, analyze multiple perspectives, and engage in evidence-based decision-making. It equips individuals with the skills to question, challenge, and understand the root causes of global challenges.

Ethical Responsibility: Global citizen education instills a sense of ethical responsibility towards others and the planet. It encourages individuals to consider the social, economic, and environmental impact of their actions, and to make choices that promote justice, equity, and sustainability.

Active Engagement: Global citizen education emphasizes the importance of active engagement and taking action to address global issues. It encourages individuals to participate in local and global initiatives, advocate for positive change, and contribute to sustainable development in their communities and beyond.

Systems Thinking: Global citizen education encourages individuals to understand the interconnectedness of global systems, including economic, social, political, and environmental systems. It promotes an understanding of how these systems interact and how they shape global challenges and opportunities.

Collaboration and Cooperation: Global citizen education highlights the significance of collaboration and cooperation in finding solutions to global problems. It promotes teamwork, dialogue, and collective action, recognizing that addressing complex global issues requires collaboration among individuals, organizations, and governments at all levels.

Encourages Environmental Sustainability: Global citizen education highlights the importance of environmental sustainability and encourages individuals to adopt environmentally responsible behaviors. It promotes an understanding of the impact of human activities on the planet and fosters a sense of responsibility towards protecting the environment. Global citizen education equips individuals with the knowledge and skills to make sustainable choices and contribute to building a more sustainable future.

Nurtures Active Citizenship and Civic Participation: Global citizenship education promotes active citizenship and encourages individuals to participate in their communities and societies. It emphasizes the importance of democratic values, human rights, and social justice. Global citizen education empowers individuals to engage in civic activities, advocate for positive change, and contribute to building inclusive, democratic, and just societies.

Prepares Individuals for a Globalized Workforce: In an increasingly interconnected world, global competence and cross-cultural skills are highly valued in the workforce. Global citizenship education equips individuals with intercultural communication skills, adaptability, and a global mindset, making them better prepared to navigate diverse work environments and collaborate with people from different cultures and backgrounds.

Strengthens Peace and Social Cohesion: Global citizenship education promotes understanding, dialogue, and peaceful coexistence among individuals and communities. It fosters a sense of shared responsibility for building peaceful and inclusive societies. By addressing issues such as social inequality, conflict resolution, and human rights, Global citizen education contributes to social cohesion and peaceful relations among diverse groups.

Global citizen education can be integrated into formal education systems, through curriculum development, teacher training, and experiential learning opportunities. It can also be promoted through non-formal education initiatives, community engagement, and awareness campaigns.

By nurturing global citizenship values and competencies, global citizen education aims to empower individuals to actively contribute to a more just, peaceful, and sustainable world. Overall, global citizenship education plays a crucial role in developing informed, responsible, and active global citizens who are equipped to address global challenges, contribute to sustainable development, and promote a more just and peaceful world.

But can education be used for something else? Something like control of the masses. It is others, or someone, pushing hidden agendas. "Since education is a social process, and there are many kinds of societies, a criterion for educational criticism and construction implies a particular social ideal."[7]

Education should never be used as a tool to control or manipulate the masses. The primary purpose of education should be to empower individuals, foster critical thinking, promote knowledge, and develop skills that enable individuals to make informed decisions, engage in constructive dialogue, and contribute positively to society. Education should encourage independent thought, creativity, and open-mindedness.

Using education to control or manipulate the masses goes against the principles of democracy, human rights, and freedom of thought. It can lead to the suppression of diverse perspectives, the propagation of propaganda, and the limitation of individual liberties. Education should strive to provide a balanced and unbiased understanding of different subjects, encouraging students to question, analyze, and form their own opinions based on evidence and rational thinking.

It is important that education systems promote autonomy, ethical values, and respect for diversity. They should encourage students to explore different ideas, challenge prevailing beliefs, and engage in critical inquiry. By nurturing independent thinking and promoting a well-rounded education, societies can cultivate informed citizens who can contribute meaningfully to their communities and work towards positive social change.

Education should be a tool for empowerment, enlightenment, and personal growth, not a means to control or manipulate the masses. It is essential to safeguard the principles of intellectual freedom, pluralism, and democratic values within education systems to ensure that education serves the best interests of individuals and society as a whole.

Unfortunately, education has been used as a tool for controlling society in various historical and contemporary contexts. Here are a few examples:

Authoritarian Regimes: Authoritarian regimes often use education to control and shape the beliefs, values, and behavior of their citizens. They may impose strict ideological frameworks, propagate propaganda, and restrict access to alternative perspectives. Education is used to promote loyalty to the ruling regime, suppress dissent, and maintain social and political control.

Indoctrination: In some cases, educational systems have been used to indoctrinate individuals with specific ideologies or extremist beliefs. This can occur in totalitarian societies, cults, or radicalized educational institutions that seek to manipulate minds and shape individuals' thoughts and behaviors to conform to a particular worldview.

Censorship and Suppression: Educational content

can be censored or manipulated to control the information accessible to students. This can involve omitting or distorting certain historical events, cultural perspectives, or scientific knowledge to shape a desired narrative and limit critical thinking. Such practices restrict individuals' access to diverse ideas and stifle intellectual freedom.

Social Conditioning: Education can be used to reinforce existing social hierarchies, perpetuate discrimination, and maintain power imbalances. Through biased curricula, unequal access to quality education, and limited opportunities for marginalized groups, societies can perpetuate systemic inequalities and control certain segments of the population.

It is important to note that while education has been used as a tool for control in some instances, this does not diminish the inherent value and potential of education to empower individuals and promote positive social change. Education, when designed with principles of inclusivity, critical thinking, and respect for diverse perspectives, can be a powerful force for enlightenment, social mobility, and the advancement of societies. It is the responsibility of governments, institutions, and individuals to ensure that education serves the best interests of individuals and promotes democratic values, intellectual freedom, and social justice.

"Now nobody would dispute that the education of

the young requires the special attention of the law-giver. Indeed, the neglect of this in states is injurious to their constitutions; for education ought to be adapted to the particular form of constitution, since the particular character belonging to each constitution both guards the constitution generally and originally establishes it—for instance the democratic spirit promotes democracy and the oligarchic spirit oligarchy; and the best spirit always causes a better constitution."[8] Even Aristotle recognized the linkage between society norms and values and the influence on the educational process. We can only hope that when education is controlling the masses, that the evidence will highlight the negativity of the educational system being utilized to teach the leaders of tomorrow. Then an educated society can rise-up and change the system.

35

UNITED NATIONS GLOBAL CLIMATE CHANGES

The United Nations has been at the forefront of global efforts to address climate change through various initiatives and frameworks. The primary framework established by the UN to tackle climate change is the United Nations Framework Convention on Climate Change (UNFCCC). The UNFCCC provides a platform for international cooperation and negotiation on climate change issues.

One of the key milestones in international climate action was the adoption of the Paris Agreement under the UNFCCC in 2015. The Paris Agreement aims to limit global warming to well below 2 degrees Celsius above pre-industrial levels and pursue efforts to limit the temperature increase to 1.5 degrees Celsius. It sets out a framework for countries to contribute to climate change mitigation and adaptation through nationally determined contributions (NDCs) and provides provisions for transparency, finance, technology transfer, and capacity building.

However, there are several obstacles and challenges in achieving global climate change goals:

Political challenges: Climate change is a global issue that requires strong political will and commitment from all countries. Differences in priorities, interests, and capabilities among nations can hinder consensus and progress in international climate negotiations. Ensuring cooperation and consensus-building among countries with diverse perspectives and priorities is a significant challenge.

Insufficient emission reduction commitments: While the Paris Agreement has brought countries together to make emission reduction commitments through their NDCs, current commitments are not sufficient to achieve the temperature targets set by the agreement. Bridging the gap between current commitments and the level of ambition needed to address climate change effectively remains a significant challenge.

Financing climate action: Mobilizing adequate financial resources to support climate change mitigation and adaptation efforts, particularly in developing countries, is a significant challenge. Developed countries have pledged to provide financial support to developing countries, but meeting these commitments and ensuring the flow of finance to climate-related projects and initiatives remains a challenge.

Technological barriers: Transitioning to a low-carbon economy requires the development and deployment of innovative and sustainable technologies. However, there are technological barriers, such as high costs, limited access to clean technologies, and the need for research and development, that hinder the widespread adoption of clean energy and sustainable practices.

Adapting to climate change impacts: Climate change is already having significant impacts on ecosystems, economies, and societies. Adapting to these impacts, such as rising sea levels, extreme weather events, and changing precipitation patterns, is a challenge, particularly for vulnerable communities and developing countries with limited resources and capacity.

Public awareness and engagement: Raising public awareness about the urgency and importance of climate change and mobilizing public support for climate action is a challenge. Overcoming skepticism, misinformation, and resistance to change can hinder efforts to implement effective climate policies and measures.

Monitoring and reporting: Ensuring transparency and accountability in climate action is crucial. Monitoring greenhouse gas emissions, tracking progress on climate commitments, and reporting accurate and reliable data require robust systems and capacities at national and international levels. Strengthening monitoring, reporting, and verification mechanisms is essential for tracking progress and enhancing trust among countries.

Addressing these obstacles requires sustained efforts and collaboration among governments, international organizations, civil society, and the private sector. It requires enhancing ambition in climate action, scaling up financial resources, fostering technology transfer and innovation, promoting climate resilience and adaptation measures, and engaging and empowering communities and individuals in climate action. The UN plays a central role in facilitating international cooperation, supporting capacity building, and driving global climate change efforts to mitigate the impacts of climate change and safeguard the planet for future generations.

But the United Nations does have an agenda for change. The United Nations (UN) has a comprehensive agenda for addressing global climate change. The key components of the UN's global climate change agenda include:

The United Nations Framework Convention on Climate Change (UNFCCC): The UNFCCC is an international treaty that provides the overarching framework for global efforts to combat climate change. It sets out the goal of stabilizing greenhouse gas concentrations in the atmosphere at a level that prevents dangerous human interference with the climate system.

The Paris Agreement: The Paris Agreement is a landmark international agreement adopted in 2015 under the UNFCCC. Its goal is to limit global warming well below 2 degrees Celsius above pre-industrial levels and pursue efforts to limit the temperature increase to 1.5 degrees Celsius. The agreement establishes a framework for countries to set and achieve their own national climate targets, known as Nationally Determined Contributions (NDCs).

Nationally Determined Contributions (NDCs): NDCs are climate action plans submitted by individual countries outlining their mitigation and adaptation strategies to address climate change. These contributions form the basis for collective global climate action under the Paris Agreement.

Sustainable Development Goals (SDGs): The SDGs, adopted by the UN in 2015, include a dedicated goal (Goal 13: Climate Action) to combat climate change and its impacts. The SDGs provide a holistic framework for addressing climate change in the context of broader sustainable development, encompassing areas such as poverty reduction, health, education, and environmental protection.

Intergovernmental Panel on Climate Change (IPCC):

The IPCC is a scientific body established by the UN and the World Meteorological Organization (WMO). It provides policymakers with comprehensive assessments of the scientific, technical, and socio-economic aspects of climate change, informing global climate action and policy decisions.

Climate Finance: The UN supports efforts to mobilize financial resources for climate change mitigation and adaptation in developing countries. This includes the Green Climate Fund, established under the UNFCCC, which aims to support developing countries in their climate action and help them adapt to the impacts of climate change.

Global Climate Conferences (COP): The UN organizes annual Conferences of the Parties (COP) to the UNFCCC, where countries gather to negotiate and discuss climate policies, actions, and progress. COP meetings provide a platform for global collaboration, knowledge-sharing, and decision-making on climate change issues.

The UN's global climate change agenda emphasizes the need for international cooperation, ambitious climate action, and the involvement of all stakeholders, including governments, businesses, civil society, and individuals. It recognizes the urgency of addressing climate change to protect the planet and ensure a sustainable future for current and future generations.

36

THE UNITED NATIONS' SUSTAINABLE DEVELOPMENT GOALS

The United Nations' Sustainable Development Goals (SDGs) are a set of 17 interconnected goals adopted by UN member states in 2015 as part of the 2030 Agenda for Sustainable Development. The SDGs provide a comprehensive framework to address global challenges and promote sustainable development in social, economic, and environmental dimensions. The goals are designed to be integrated and balanced, recognizing the interlinkages among various issues and the need for a holistic approach. The SDGs cover a wide range of areas, including poverty eradication, education, gender equality, climate action, sustainable cities, and more. Here is an overview of the 17 SDGs:

1. No Poverty: End poverty in all its forms and dimensions.

2. Zero Hunger: Achieve food security, improve nutrition, and promote sustainable agriculture.

3. Good Health and Well-Being: Ensure healthy lives and promote well-being for all at all ages.

4. Quality Education: Ensure inclusive and equitable quality education and promote lifelong learning opportunities for all.

5. Gender Equality: Achieve gender equality and empower all women and girls.

6. Clean Water and Sanitation: Ensure availability and sustainable management of water and sanitation for all.

7. Affordable and Clean Energy: Ensure access to affordable, reliable, sustainable, and modern energy for all.

8. Decent Work and Economic Growth: Promote sustained, inclusive, and sustainable economic growth, full and productive employment, and decent work for all.

9. Industry, Innovation, and Infrastructure: Build resilient infrastructure, promote inclusive and sustainable industrialization, and foster innovation.

10. Reduced Inequalities: Reduce inequality within and among countries.

11. Sustainable Cities and Communities: Make cities and human settlements inclusive, safe, resilient, and sustainable.

12. Responsible Consumption and Production: Ensure sustainable consumption and production patterns.

13. Climate Action: Take urgent action to combat climate change and its impacts.

14. Life Below Water: Conserve and sustainably use the oceans, seas, and marine resources for sustainable development.

15. Life on Land: Protect, restore, and promote sustainable use of terrestrial ecosystems, sustainably manage forests, combat desertification, halt and reverse land degradation, and halt biodiversity loss.

16. Peace, Justice, and Strong Institutions: Promote peaceful and inclusive societies, provide access to justice for all, and build effective, accountable, and inclusive institutions at all levels.

17. Partnerships for the Goals: Strengthen the means of implementation and revitalize the global partnership for sustainable development.

These goals serve as a blueprint for countries, organizations, and individuals to work towards a more sustainable and equitable future. Achieving the SDGs requires collaboration, innovation, and collective action at local, national, and global levels.

37

THE UNITED NATIONS' SDG LINKED TO CLIMATE CHANGES

The United Nations' Sustainable Development Goal (SDG) that is most directly linked to climate change is SDG 13: Climate Action. SDG 13 recognizes the urgent need to address climate change, as it poses significant challenges to sustainable development and has wide-ranging impacts on ecosystems, economies, and societies. The goal emphasizes the importance of adaptation to climate-related hazards, reducing greenhouse gas emissions, and building resilience to climate change impacts.

Achieving SDG 13 requires a global effort to mitigate greenhouse gas emissions, transition to clean and renewable energy sources, promote sustainable practices in industries, enhance climate change education and awareness, and support vulnerable communities in adapting to climate change impacts.

The goal aligns with the Paris Agreement, an international treaty aimed at limiting global warming to well below 2 degrees Celsius above pre-industrial levels and pursuing efforts to limit the temperature increase to 1.5 degrees Celsius. It emphasizes the need for global cooperation, policy frameworks, technology transfer, and financial support to address climate change effectively.

SDG 13 has several targets to guide action on climate change, including:

Mitigation: Strengthening resilience and adaptive capacity to climate-related hazards and natural disasters in all countries.

Adaptation: Integrating climate change measures into national policies, strategies, and planning.

Finance: Mobilizing and significantly increasing the availability of financial resources to address climate change.

Education and Awareness: Promoting climate change education, awareness, and capacity-building initiatives.

International Cooperation: Enhancing international cooperation to support developing countries in their efforts to combat climate change.

SDG 13 recognizes the global nature of climate change and the need for coordinated action at local, national, and international levels. It emphasizes the importance of reducing greenhouse gas emissions, promoting renewable energy, and transitioning to sustainable and low-carbon economies. Additionally, it calls for increased resilience to climate impacts, including adaptation measures to protect vulnerable communities and ecosystems.

Achieving SDG 13 is closely tied to other goals within the 2030 Agenda. Climate change has cross-cutting implications for poverty eradication (SDG 1), health (SDG 3), water and sanitation (SDG 6), sustainable cities (SDG 11), life below water (SDG 14) and biodiversity conservation (SDG 15), among others. Addressing climate change is integral to ensuring sustainable development and the well-being of present and future generations.

Efforts to address climate change under SDG 13 involve policy and regulatory frameworks, technological innovations, financial mechanisms, capacity building, and international cooperation. The aim is to limit global warming, build climate resilience, and transition to a sustainable and low-carbon future.

~ 38 ~

SDG 1: POVERTY
ERADICATION

The "No Poverty" goal recognizes that poverty is a complex issue with multidimensional aspects beyond income or financial resources. It includes addressing social exclusion, access to basic services (such as education, healthcare, clean water, and sanitation), and opportunities for economic empowerment.

Achieving SDG 1 requires coordinated efforts from governments, international organizations, civil society, and the private sector. It involves implementing inclusive and sustainable economic growth strategies, promoting social protection systems, enhancing access to quality education and healthcare, ensuring equal rights and opportunities for all, and addressing the structural causes and inequalities that perpetuate poverty.

By working towards poverty eradication, the SDGs aim

to create a more just, equitable, and sustainable world where everyone has access to the necessary resources and opportunities to thrive and improve their quality of life.

Poverty eradication and climate control are interconnected issues that need to be addressed together for sustainable development. Here's how they are linked:

Climate Change Impacts on Poverty: Climate change exacerbates poverty and inequality by disproportionately affecting vulnerable populations. Extreme weather events, such as droughts, floods, and storms, can destroy livelihoods, damage infrastructure, and disrupt agricultural productivity. Climate change also affects access to natural resources, such as clean water and fertile land, which are essential for the livelihoods of many poor communities.

Poverty Impedes Climate Action: Poverty can hinder efforts to mitigate and adapt to climate change. Limited financial resources, inadequate infrastructure, and lack of access to clean energy can make it challenging for impoverished communities to transition to low-carbon and climate-resilient practices. Poverty can also result in limited capacity for disaster preparedness and response, making vulnerable populations more susceptible to the impacts of climate change.

Co-Benefits of Climate Action: Taking action on climate change can have co-benefits for poverty eradication. For example, investing in renewable energy can improve access to affordable and clean energy for marginalized communities. Climate-resilient agriculture practices can enhance food security and income opportunities for smallholder farmers. Sustainable transport solutions can increase access to education and job opportunities for disadvantaged populations.

Sustainable Development Pathways: Addressing poverty and climate change in an integrated manner is crucial for achieving sustainable development. Sustainable development pathways aim to uplift people out of poverty while reducing greenhouse gas emissions and building resilience to climate change. This requires inclusive and equitable economic growth, social protection systems, access to education and healthcare, and sustainable resource management.

Policy Integration: Policymakers are increasingly recognizing the interlinkages between poverty eradication and climate action. Integrating climate considerations into poverty reduction strategies and national development plans can lead to more effective and coordinated efforts. Climate financing mechanisms, such as the Green Climate Fund, aim to support developing countries in pursuing low-carbon and climate-resilient development pathways while addressing poverty eradication.

By addressing poverty eradication and climate change

together, it is possible to achieve more sustainable and equitable outcomes. This approach involves empowering vulnerable communities, providing access to resources and opportunities, promoting sustainable livelihoods, and ensuring that climate actions are designed to be socially inclusive and environmentally sustainable.

~ 39 ~

SDG 3: HEALTH

SDG 3 aims to ensure healthy lives and promote well-being for all, addressing various aspects of health, including maternal and child health, infectious diseases, non-communicable diseases, mental health, substance abuse, and road safety. It emphasizes the importance of access to healthcare services, prevention, and promotion of well-being at all stages of life.

Achieving SDG 3 involves strengthening health systems, improving healthcare infrastructure and services, increasing access to affordable and essential medicines, promoting health education and awareness, and addressing social determinants of health. It also involves tackling global health challenges, such as communicable diseases, epidemics, and the impact of environmental factors on health.

SDG 3 is closely interconnected with other goals, as good health and well-being are essential for sustainable development. It contributes to poverty reduction, gender equality, quality education, and economic growth by ensuring that individuals can lead healthy and productive lives.

SDG 3 is focused on ensuring healthy lives and promoting well-being for all at all ages. While the direct link between SDG 3 and climate change may not be immediately evident, there are several ways in which climate change impacts health and intersects with this goal:

Direct Health Impacts: Climate change can lead to an increase in extreme weather events, such as heatwaves, hurricanes, and floods. These events can cause injuries, loss of life, and displacement of communities, resulting in direct health consequences. Additionally, heatwaves can exacerbate existing health conditions and lead to heat-related illnesses, while changes in rainfall patterns can affect water quality and increase the risk of waterborne diseases.

Infectious Diseases: Climate change can influence the distribution and prevalence of infectious diseases. Rising temperatures, altered precipitation patterns, and changes in ecosystems can impact the breeding, behavior, and geographic range of disease vectors like mosquitoes and ticks. This can lead to the spread of vector-borne diseases such as malaria, dengue fever, Lyme disease, and others.

Food Security and Nutrition: Climate change can affect food production and availability, leading to food insecurity and malnutrition. Changes in temperature, rainfall patterns, and extreme weather events can disrupt agricultural systems, impacting crop yields and livestock production. This can contribute to food shortages, inadequate nutrition, and increased vulnerability to disease.

Mental Health: Climate change-related events, such as natural disasters and loss of livelihoods, can have significant psychological and emotional impacts on individuals and communities. The stress, trauma, and displacement caused by these events can lead to mental health issues and psychosocial challenges.

Climate Policies and Co-Benefits: Taking action on climate change can have positive impacts on health. Policies aimed at reducing greenhouse gas emissions, promoting clean energy, and improving air quality can lead to co-benefits for human health. For example, transitioning from fossil fuels to renewable energy sources can reduce air pollution and respiratory diseases.

Adaptation and Resilience: Building resilience to climate change is essential for protecting human health. This involves implementing measures such as early warning systems, improved disaster response, access to clean water and sanitation, and healthcare infrastructure that can withstand climate-related hazards.

Addressing climate change is therefore crucial for achieving SDG 3 and ensuring good health and well-being for all. Integrated approaches that consider the health implications of climate change and promote climate-resilient healthcare systems, sustainable food production, and disaster preparedness can contribute to achieving the targets of SDG 3.

SDG 6: WATER AND SANITATION

The United Nations' Sustainable Development Goal 6 (SDG 6) is to ensure clean water and sanitation for all. This goal aims to achieve universal access to safe and affordable drinking water, adequate sanitation facilities, and improved hygiene practices. However, achieving clean water and sanitation faces several obstacles. Here are some key challenges:

Lack of access to clean water: Many people around the world still lack access to safe and clean drinking water. Limited infrastructure, water scarcity, pollution, and geographic constraints can hinder access to clean water sources, particularly in rural and remote areas.

Inadequate sanitation facilities: Access to proper sanitation facilities, such as toilets and waste management systems, remains a challenge for a significant portion of the global population. Lack of sanitation infrastructure, poor hygiene practices, and cultural barriers contribute to inadequate sanitation and pose health risks.

Water pollution and contamination: Water sources can be polluted by industrial discharge, agricultural runoff, improper waste management, and inadequate wastewater treatment. Contaminated water can lead to waterborne diseases, posing risks to public health and the environment.

Water scarcity and competing demands: Water scarcity is a growing global concern, particularly in arid and semi-arid regions. Population growth, climate change, increased water consumption, and competing water demands for agriculture, industry, and domestic use exacerbate the challenge of ensuring sufficient water resources for all.

Gender inequality and social norms: Women and girls are often disproportionately affected by inadequate access to clean water and sanitation. Gender inequalities, cultural norms, and social roles can limit women's involvement in decision-making processes and their ability to access and manage water resources.

Poor sanitation and hygiene practices: Inadequate sanitation facilities and poor hygiene practices contribute to the spread of waterborne diseases such as diarrhea, cholera, and hepatitis. Promoting proper sanitation and hygiene behaviors, including handwashing, requires education, behavior change campaigns, and improved infrastructure.

Climate change impacts: Climate change poses significant challenges to water resources and sanitation. Rising temperatures, changing precipitation patterns, and extreme weather events can affect water availability, quality, and sanitation infrastructure, exacerbating water-related challenges.

Limited infrastructure and maintenance: Insufficient investment in water and sanitation infrastructure, particularly in marginalized and underserved areas, hampers progress in achieving clean water and sanitation goals. Lack of maintenance, aging infrastructure, and inadequate funding can lead to service disruptions and deteriorating water and sanitation facilities.

Financial constraints and affordability: Ensuring clean water and sanitation services require financial resources for infrastructure development, operation, and maintenance. Limited funding, particularly in low-income communities and countries, can make it challenging to provide affordable access to clean water and sanitation facilities.

Governance and institutional capacity: Effective water resource management and sanitation require robust governance frameworks, institutional capacity, and stakeholder participation. Weak institutional arrangements, lack of coordination, and limited local capacity can hinder progress in achieving clean water and sanitation goals.

Addressing these obstacles requires a comprehensive approach that includes improving infrastructure and water management systems, promoting sustainable water use practices, enhancing sanitation infrastructure and behavior change campaigns, investing in research and innovation, strengthening governance and institutional capacity, and fostering international cooperation and partnerships. It also requires addressing social and cultural factors, promoting gender equality, and ensuring the involvement of local communities in decision-making processes related to water and sanitation.

~ 41 ~

SDG 7: AFFORDABLE AND CLEAN ENERGY

SDG 7 recognizes the importance of affordable and clean energy in eradicating poverty, promoting economic growth, improving living conditions, and addressing climate change. It emphasizes the need for universal access to reliable and modern energy services, promoting the use of renewable energy sources, and increasing energy efficiency.

In 2018, air pollution from fossil fuels caused $2.9 trillion in health and economic costs, about $8 billion a day.

Switching to clean sources of energy, such as wind and solar, thus helps address not only climate change, but also air pollution, and health.

The United Nations' Sustainable Development Goal 7 (SDG 7) is to ensure affordable and clean energy for all.

This goal aims to provide access to reliable, sustainable, and modern energy services while promoting renewable energy sources and energy efficiency. However, achieving affordable and clean energy faces several challenges. Here are some key obstacles:

Lack of access to electricity: Many people around the world still lack access to electricity, particularly in rural and remote areas. Limited infrastructure, high costs, and geographical barriers can impede efforts to provide affordable and clean energy to underserved populations.

Dependence on fossil fuels: Fossil fuels continue to dominate the global energy mix, contributing to greenhouse gas emissions and air pollution. Transitioning away from fossil fuels to renewable energy sources is necessary but can be hindered by vested interests, political barriers, and existing infrastructure.

High upfront costs: Clean energy technologies such as solar panels, wind turbines, and energy storage systems often have high upfront costs, making them less affordable for individuals, communities, and developing countries. Financial barriers can hinder the widespread adoption of clean energy solutions.

Limited investment and financing: Insufficient investment and financing for clean energy projects can impede their development and deployment. Inadequate access to affordable capital, lack of risk mitigation mechanisms, and policy uncertainties can discourage investors from supporting clean energy initiatives.

Grid limitations and infrastructure challenges: Integrating renewable energy into existing power grids and infrastructure can pose technical challenges. Grid limitations, transmission losses, and the need for grid expansion can hinder the scalability and reliability of clean energy systems.

Technology and innovation gaps: Advancements in clean energy technologies, energy storage, and grid integration are essential for achieving affordable and clean energy. However, technological barriers, limited research and development, and inadequate knowledge sharing can slow down progress in this area.

Policy and regulatory barriers: Inconsistent or inadequate policy frameworks and regulations can impede the development and deployment of clean energy solutions. Unclear or unfavorable policies, lack of supportive incentives, and bureaucratic hurdles can hinder investments in renewable energy projects.

Energy inequality and social considerations: Achieving affordable and clean energy for all requires addressing energy inequality and ensuring that vulnerable and marginalized populations are not left behind.

Social, cultural, and gender-related barriers can impact energy access and usage patterns.

Capacity building and skills development: Building the necessary human capacity and skills for clean energy development, operation, and maintenance is crucial. Limited technical expertise, training opportunities, and knowledge dissemination can hinder the effective implementation and management of clean energy systems.

Global cooperation and coordination: Achieving affordable and clean energy requires international cooperation, knowledge sharing, and coordinated efforts among countries, organizations, and stakeholders. Disparities in priorities, competing interests, and lack of collaboration can impede progress in this area.

Addressing these obstacles requires a multi-faceted approach that includes policy reforms, increased investments in clean energy research and development, financial support mechanisms, capacity building initiatives, and strengthened international cooperation. It also requires engagement with local communities, empowering them to participate in decision-making processes and benefit from affordable and clean energy solutions. By working towards SDG 7, the aim is to ensure that affordable, reliable, sustainable, and modern energy is accessible to all, contributing to poverty reduction, environmental sustainability, and improved quality of life for individuals and communities.

~ 42 ~

SDG 9: INDUSTRY, INNOVATION, AND INFRASTRUCTURE

SDG 9 recognizes the importance of sustainable infrastructure, inclusive industrialization, and technological innovation in fostering economic growth, creating employment opportunities, and promoting sustainable development. It highlights the need for quality infrastructure that supports economic activities, facilitates connectivity, and ensures access to basic services for all.

By promoting sustainable industrial practices and innovation, societies can reduce resource consumption, minimize environmental impacts, adopt cleaner technologies, and improve productivity. Inclusive industrialization can also contribute to poverty reduction and socioeconomic empowerment.

SDG 9 is interconnected with other SDGs, such as

affordable and clean energy
(SDG 7), sustainable cities and communities (SDG 11), responsible consumption and production (SDG 12), and climate action (SDG 13).

By working towards SDG 9, the aim is to build resilient infrastructure, promote inclusive and sustainable industrialization, and foster innovation, contributing to economic development, job creation, and sustainable growth while minimizing negative environmental impacts.

The United Nations' Sustainable Development Goal 9 (SDG 9) focuses on building resilient infrastructure, promoting inclusive and sustainable industrialization, and fostering innovation. This goal recognizes the crucial role of industry, innovation, and infrastructure in driving economic growth, promoting sustainable development, and addressing societal challenges. However, achieving SDG 9 faces several obstacles. Here are some key challenges:

Infrastructure gaps: Many regions, particularly in developing countries, face significant infrastructure gaps in areas such as transportation, energy, water and sanitation, and information and communication technology (ICT). Limited access to reliable and efficient infrastructure hampers economic development, hinders social progress, and undermines resilience to shocks and disasters.

Sustainable and inclusive industrialization: Industrialization plays a critical role in driving economic growth and job creation. However, traditional industrial practices often have negative environmental and social impacts, including pollution, resource depletion, and labor rights violations. Achieving sustainable and inclusive industrialization requires transitioning to cleaner and more resource-efficient production methods, promoting responsible business practices, and ensuring decent work conditions.

Technological advancements and innovation: Rapid technological advancements, including digitalization, automation, and artificial intelligence, have the potential to revolutionize industries and create new opportunities. However, ensuring that these advancements are harnessed for sustainable development and benefit all segments of society is a challenge. Bridging the digital divide, promoting access to and affordability of technology, and fostering innovation in sectors critical for sustainable development, such as renewable energy and sustainable agriculture, are key challenges.

Financing sustainable infrastructure: The scale of investment required to develop sustainable infrastructure and support innovation efforts is significant. Mobilizing adequate financial resources, including public and private investments, for infrastructure development and technology adoption in developing countries is a challenge. Enhancing access to finance, creating conducive investment environments, and leveraging innovative financing mechanisms are crucial for bridging the financing gap.

Capacity building and technology transfer: Developing countries often face limited capacity and technological know-how to effectively plan, develop, and maintain infrastructure and adopt innovative practices. Strengthening capacity-building efforts, promoting technology transfer, and facilitating knowledge-sharing and collaboration among countries and stakeholders are important challenges in achieving SDG 9.

Environmental considerations: Developing sustainable infrastructure and fostering innovation must go hand in hand with environmental considerations. Ensuring that infrastructure projects and industrial practices are aligned with climate goals, promote energy efficiency, reduce resource consumption, and minimize environmental impacts is crucial. Balancing economic development with environmental sustainability requires robust environmental regulations, enforcement mechanisms, and green technology adoption.

Inclusive and equitable access: Ensuring that the benefits of infrastructure development, industrialization, and innovation reach all segments of society, including marginalized communities, is essential for achieving inclusive and sustainable development. Overcoming inequalities in access to basic services, digital connectivity, and economic opportunities is a challenge that requires targeted policies, social inclusion measures, and empowerment of marginalized groups.

Addressing these obstacles requires a comprehensive and integrated approach that involves governments, international organizations, businesses, civil society, and local communities. It involves promoting sustainable infrastructure planning and development, fostering innovation ecosystems, strengthening institutional capacities, facilitating technology transfer, promoting responsible business practices, and enhancing international cooperation. The UN plays a central role in facilitating dialogue, knowledge-sharing, and coordination among stakeholders to advance sustainable industry, innovation, and infrastructure for the benefit of all.

~ 43 ~

SDG 11: SUSTAINABLE CITIES AND COMMUNITIES

The United Nations' Sustainable Development Goal 11 (SDG 11) is to make cities and human settlements inclusive, safe, resilient, and sustainable. It recognizes that urban areas face various challenges, such as rapid population growth, inadequate housing, inadequate basic services, traffic congestion, pollution, and vulnerability to natural disasters.

To achieve SDG 11, efforts are needed to improve housing and living conditions, enhance urban planning and management, provide affordable and sustainable transport options, protect cultural and natural heritage, reduce the environmental impact of cities, enhance disaster resilience, and ensure access to safe and inclusive public spaces.

Sustainable cities and communities contribute to several other SDGs, including poverty eradication (SDG 1), good health and well-being (SDG 3), quality education (SDG 4), gender equality (SDG 5), clean water and sanitation (SDG 6), affordable and clean energy (SDG 7), decent work and economic growth (SDG 8), and climate action (SDG 13).

By working towards SDG 11, the aim is to create cities and communities that are inclusive, safe, resilient, and sustainable, providing quality living conditions for all residents and promoting sustainable development in urban areas.

1 billion people live in urban slums.

1.5 billion people live in countries affected by repeated cycles of violence.

In the past decade, the number of people affected by natural disasters tripled to 2 billion.

Low-income countries have accounted for only 9% of the disaster events but 48% of fatalities in the last 45 years.

The burden of disasters, conflict, crime, and violence falls disproportionately on the poor.

This goal focuses on creating sustainable cities and communities that are environmentally friendly, socially inclusive, economically vibrant, and resilient to various challenges. However, achieving sustainable cities and communities faces several obstacles. Here are some key challenges:

Rapid urbanization: The world is experiencing unprecedented urbanization, with the majority of the global population living in cities. Rapid urban growth can strain existing infrastructure, housing, services, and resources, making it challenging to ensure sustainable development.

Informal settlements and slums: Many cities around the world have informal settlements and slums characterized by inadequate housing, limited access to basic services, and poor living conditions. Overcoming the challenges associated with informal settlements requires efforts to provide affordable housing, improve infrastructure, and enhance social services.

Inadequate urban planning: Ineffective urban planning can lead to unsustainable development patterns, including urban sprawl, lack of public spaces, inadequate transportation systems, and segregated communities. Integrated and participatory urban planning is essential for creating sustainable cities and communities.

Traffic congestion and air pollution: Increasing motorization and traffic congestion contribute to air pollution, greenhouse gas emissions, and health problems in cities. Promoting sustainable transportation options, such as public transit, cycling, and walking, can help alleviate traffic congestion and reduce air pollution.

Inequality and social exclusion: Cities can face challenges related to inequality, social exclusion, and unequal access to opportunities. Addressing social disparities, promoting inclusive urban development, and ensuring affordable housing, healthcare, education, and social services are crucial for sustainable cities and communities.

Climate change impacts: Cities are particularly vulnerable to the impacts of climate change, including rising temperatures, extreme weather events, and sea-level rise. Building resilient infrastructure, implementing climate change adaptation measures, and reducing greenhouse gas emissions are essential for sustainable urban development.

Waste management and pollution: Managing solid waste, wastewater, and pollution in cities is a significant challenge. Inadequate waste management systems, improper disposal practices, and pollution from industries can harm the environment and public health. Adopting sustainable waste management practices and promoting circular economy approaches can contribute to a cleaner and healthier urban environment.

Limited access to basic services: Ensuring universal access to basic services such as clean water, sanitation, electricity, healthcare, and education remains a challenge in many cities. Enhancing infrastructure, improving service delivery, and addressing affordability barriers are necessary for sustainable urban development.

Governance and stakeholder engagement: Effective governance, stakeholder engagement, and participatory decision-making processes are crucial for sustainable cities and communities. Engaging local communities, civil society organizations, and the private sector in urban planning and development can lead to more inclusive and sustainable outcomes.

Financing sustainable urban development: Adequate financing is essential for implementing sustainable urban development projects and initiatives. Limited financial resources, budget constraints, and insufficient investment in sustainable infrastructure can hinder progress in achieving sustainable cities and communities.

Addressing these obstacles requires a comprehensive approach that integrates environmental, social, and economic considerations into urban planning and development. It requires collaboration among governments, local authorities, communities, and various stakeholders to implement sustainable policies, improve infrastructure, promote affordable housing, enhance transportation systems, and strengthen resilience to climate change and other challenges.

SDG 12: RESPONSIBLE CONSUMPTION AND PRODUCTION

SDG 12: responsible consumption and productions is about ensuring sustainable consumption and production patterns, which is key to sustain the livelihoods of current and future generations. After basic needs are met, consumers begin buying items for social status; as people try to acquire more and more status, more and more expensive status products are needed. Producing all the products that we buy and consume generates climate-changing greenhouse gas emissions.

The United Nations' Sustainable Development Goal 12 (SDG 12) is focused on ensuring responsible consumption and production patterns. This goal recognizes the need to decouple economic growth from environmental degradation, promote resource efficiency, and promote sustainable lifestyles. However, achieving SDG 12 faces several obstacles. Here are some key challenges:

Unsustainable consumption patterns: Current patterns of consumption, particularly in developed countries, often involve high levels of resource consumption, waste generation, and environmental impact. Addressing unsustainable consumption patterns requires promoting awareness and behavioral change, encouraging sustainable consumer choices, and promoting circular economy approaches that minimize waste and maximize resource efficiency.

Production practices and supply chains: Many production practices, particularly in industries such as manufacturing and agriculture, contribute to environmental degradation, resource depletion, and social inequalities. Ensuring responsible production practices and promoting sustainable supply chains require integrating sustainability considerations into business operations, adopting clean technologies and practices, and ensuring fair and ethical treatment of workers throughout the supply chain.

Waste management: Inadequate waste management systems and practices contribute to pollution, land degradation, and resource wastage. Addressing waste management challenges requires implementing efficient waste collection, recycling, and disposal systems, promoting the principles of reduce, reuse, and recycle, and fostering a shift towards a circular economy where waste is minimized, and materials are kept in use for as long as possible.

Access to sustainable products and services: Limited availability and affordability of sustainable products and services hinder the transition to responsible consumption and production. Overcoming barriers to access sustainable options, such as renewable energy, eco-friendly products, and sustainable agriculture, requires promoting market incentives, creating supportive policy frameworks, and enhancing consumer education and awareness.

Global inequality and consumption disparities: Global inequality in access to resources and consumption patterns presents a challenge in achieving responsible consumption and production. Reducing disparities and promoting sustainable development for all requires addressing poverty, promoting inclusive economic growth, and ensuring equitable access to resources and opportunities.

Policy and regulatory frameworks: Inadequate policy and regulatory frameworks hinder the adoption of sustainable consumption and production practices. Strengthening policy coherence, promoting sustainable public procurement, providing incentives for sustainable business practices, and enforcing regulations effectively are key challenges in achieving responsible consumption and production.

Collaboration and stakeholder engagement: Transitioning towards responsible consumption and production requires collaboration among governments, businesses, civil society organizations, and consumers. Building partnerships, fostering multi-stakeholder engagement, and promoting collective action are crucial for driving systemic change and achieving SDG 12.

Addressing these obstacles requires a multi-faceted approach that involves a combination of policy measures, awareness campaigns, technological advancements, and stakeholder engagement. It requires aligning economic incentives with sustainable development objectives, promoting sustainable business models, investing in research and development of clean technologies, and empowering consumers to make informed choices. The UN plays a vital role in facilitating international cooperation, setting targets and indicators for responsible consumption and production, and promoting best practices and knowledge sharing among countries and stakeholders.

~ 45 ~

SDG 14: LIFE BELOW WATER

The United Nations' Sustainable Development Goal 14 (SDG 14) is focused on conserving and sustainably using the oceans, seas, and marine resources. SDG 14 recognizes the importance of healthy and productive oceans for sustainable development. It highlights the need to protect marine ecosystems, reduce pollution, address ocean acidification, combat overfishing and destructive fishing practices, conserve coastal and marine areas, and support the sustainable use of marine resources.

To achieve SDG 14, efforts are required to promote sustainable fishing practices, strengthen marine conservation and protected areas, reduce marine pollution, enhance scientific research and cooperation, address the impacts of climate change on oceans, and promote sustainable tourism and economic activities that rely on marine resources.

Sustainable management of oceans and marine re-sources contributes to several other SDGs, including pov-erty eradication (SDG 1), zero hunger (SDG 2), good health and well-being (SDG 3), clean water and sanitation (SDG 6), sustainable cities and communities (SDG 11), climate action (SDG 13), and life on land (SDG 15).

By working towards SDG 14, the aim is to conserve and sustainably use the oceans, seas, and marine resources for present and future generations, ensuring their health and productivity while supporting sustainable development and livelihoods of communities that depend on marine ecosystems.

The oceans cover more than 70 percent of the sur-face of our planet and play a key role in supporting life on earth.

Oceans play an integral role in climate change mit-igation, absorbing some 23% of human-caused carbon dioxide emissions and more than 90% of the excess heat created by human-caused greenhouse gases.

Climate Change disrupts ocean patterns, and thus fish distribution and migration patterns, with a direct risk to food security of fish-dependent coastal com-munities.

This goal, known as "Life Below Water," aims to pro-tect marine ecosystems, promote sustainable fisheries, reduce marine pollution, and address the impacts of climate change on oceans. However, achieving SDG 14 faces several obstacles. Here are some key challenges:

Overfishing and unsustainable fishing practices: Overfishing and destructive fishing practices, such as bottom trawling and illegal, unreported, and unregulated fishing, pose significant threats to marine biodiversity and the sustainability of fish stocks. Effective fisheries management, including the establishment of marine protected areas and the promotion of sustainable fishing practices, is essential to address these challenges.

Marine pollution: Marine pollution, including plastic waste, oil spills, chemical pollutants, and nutrient runoff, degrades marine ecosystems and harms marine life. Reducing pollution from various sources, improving waste management systems, and promoting sustainable production and consumption patterns are crucial for protecting life below water.

Coastal habitat loss and degradation: Coastal habitats, such as coral reefs, mangroves, and seagrass beds, are vital for marine biodiversity and provide important ecosystem services. However, these habitats are under threat from coastal development, pollution, climate change impacts, and destructive practices. Protecting and restoring coastal habitats are key challenges for ensuring the health and resilience of marine ecosystems.

Ocean acidification and warming: The increasing concentration of carbon dioxide in the atmosphere leads to ocean acidification, which negatively affects marine organisms, particularly those with calcium carbonate structures like coral reefs and shellfish. Additionally, rising ocean temperatures contribute to coral bleaching, shifting species distributions, and altered marine ecosystems. Mitigating climate change and reducing greenhouse gas emissions are critical for addressing these challenges.

Lack of marine governance and enforcement: The effective governance and enforcement of regulations and policies related to marine conservation and sustainable use are often lacking. Strengthening international cooperation, improving governance frameworks, enhancing monitoring and enforcement capacities, and promoting stakeholder engagement are essential for achieving SDG 14.

Limited capacity and resources: Many countries, particularly small island developing states (SIDS) and least developed countries (LDCs), face limited capacity and resources to address the challenges related to life below water. Building institutional and technical capacities, mobilizing financial resources, and providing technical assistance and knowledge sharing are crucial for supporting these countries in achieving SDG 14.

Lack of public awareness and engagement: Raising public awareness and fostering behavioral change are important for promoting sustainable practices and conservation efforts. Increasing public understanding of the value of marine ecosystems, the impacts of human activities, and the importance of individual and collective actions is essential for achieving SDG 14.

Addressing these obstacles requires a combination of measures, including improved fisheries management, reduction of marine pollution, conservation and restoration of coastal habitats, climate change mitigation and adaptation, strengthened governance frameworks, enhanced capacity building and financing, and widespread education and awareness campaigns. Collaboration among governments, international organizations, civil society, and the private sector is crucial to effectively address the challenges and achieve sustainable management of life below water.

SDG 15: LIFE ON LAND

The United Nations' Sustainable Development Goal 15 (SDG 15) emphasizes the importance of protecting and restoring terrestrial ecosystems, conserving biodiversity, and combating land degradation. It recognizes the vital role that forests, wetlands, mountains, and other ecosystems play in supporting life on land, providing essential ecosystem services, and contributing to sustainable development.

Achieving SDG 15 requires efforts to promote sustainable land management, protect and restore ecosystems, combat deforestation and desertification, conserve biodiversity and endangered species, and address the drivers of habitat loss and wildlife trafficking.

Sustainable land and ecosystem management contribute to several other SDGs, including poverty eradication (SDG 1), zero hunger (SDG 2), good health and well-being

(SDG 3), clean water and sanitation (SDG 6), sustainable cities and communities (SDG 11), climate action (SDG 13), and life below water (SDG 14).

By working towards SDG 15, the aim is to ensure the conservation and sustainable use of terrestrial ecosystems, protect biodiversity, combat land degradation, and promote sustainable land management practices, fostering the well-being of ecosystems, wildlife, and communities that depend on them.

More frequent and intense drought, storms, heat waves, rising sea levels, melting glaciers, and warming oceans can directly harm animals, destroy the places they live, and wreak havoc on people's livelihoods and communities.

This goal, known as "Life on Land," aims to conserve and sustainably manage forests, halt land degradation, halt biodiversity loss, and promote the restoration of degraded land. However, achieving SDG 15 faces several obstacles. Here are some key challenges:

Deforestation and habitat loss: Deforestation, primarily driven by agriculture, logging, infrastructure development, and urbanization, is a major challenge for preserving terrestrial ecosystems. The loss of forests and other natural habitats leads to the loss of biodiversity, increased carbon emissions, and disruptions to ecosystem services. Implementing sustainable land-use practices, protecting forests, and promoting reforestation and afforestation are critical for addressing deforestation and habitat loss.

Land degradation and desertification: Land degradation, including soil erosion, desertification, and degradation of rangelands, poses significant threats to the health and productivity of terrestrial ecosystems. Unsustainable agriculture practices, improper land management, and climate change contribute to land degradation. Implementing sustainable land management practices, promoting soil conservation, and restoring degraded lands are key challenges for halting and reversing land degradation.

Biodiversity loss and species extinction: The loss of biodiversity is a pressing concern for life on land. Habitat destruction, pollution, invasive species, over-exploitation of resources, and climate change contribute to the extinction of plant and animal species. Protecting and conserving biodiversity, establishing, and effectively managing protected areas, and promoting sustainable use of natural resources are vital for addressing biodiversity loss.

Illegal wildlife trade: The illegal trade in wildlife, including endangered species and their parts, poses a significant threat to biodiversity conservation. It contributes to the decline of many species and undermines conservation efforts. Strengthening law enforcement, enhancing international cooperation, raising public awareness, and addressing the root causes of illegal wildlife trade are key challenges for combating this issue.

Climate change impacts: Climate change has far-reaching effects on terrestrial ecosystems, including shifts in temperature and precipitation patterns, altered habitat suitability, increased frequency and intensity of extreme weather events, and sea-level rise. Mitigating climate change through greenhouse gas emissions reduction and adaptation measures is crucial for protecting life on land and ensuring the resilience of terrestrial ecosystems.

Land rights and governance: Securing land rights and ensuring effective land governance are important challenges for sustainable land management. Inadequate land tenure systems, unclear land rights, conflicts over land resources, and weak governance structures hinder efforts to protect and sustainably manage land. Strengthening land governance, promoting inclusive land rights, and engaging local communities in decision-making processes are essential for achieving SDG 15.

Capacity building and financing: Many countries, particularly developing nations, face limited capacity and financial resources to address the challenges related to life on land. Building institutional and technical capacities, mobilizing financial resources, and providing technical assistance and knowledge sharing are crucial for supporting these countries in achieving SDG 15.

Addressing these obstacles requires a combination of measures, including sustainable land-use practices, reforestation and restoration of degraded lands, conservation of biodiversity and protected areas, climate change mitigation and adaptation, improved land governance, enhanced law enforcement, and capacity building. Collaboration among governments, international organizations, civil society, indigenous peoples, and the private sector is essential to effectively address the challenges and achieve sustainable management of life on land.

~ 47 ~

NEWLY EMERGING OPPORTUNITIES – OUTER SPACE

"Newly Emerging Opportunities - Outer Space" refers to the potential benefits, advancements, and opportunities that arise from exploring and utilizing outer space. This concept recognizes that space exploration, satellite technology, and space-based activities can present new possibilities and innovations for various sectors.

Some of the emerging opportunities in outer space include:

Satellite Communication and Connectivity: Satellites enable global communication and provide internet connectivity to remote and underserved regions. They facilitate telecommunications, broadcasting, remote sensing, and data transmission, enhancing connectivity and bridging the digital divide.

Earth Observation and Remote Sensing: Satellites equipped with sensors and cameras allow for Earth observation and remote sensing. They provide data on weather patterns, natural disasters, land use, environmental changes, and resource management, supporting various applications in agriculture, forestry, urban planning, and climate monitoring.

Navigation and Global Positioning Systems (GPS): Satellite-based navigation systems, such as GPS, enable precise positioning, navigation, and timing services. They support transportation, logistics, mapping, and geospatial applications, improving efficiency and accuracy in various industries.

Space Tourism and Exploration: The emerging field of space tourism offers opportunities for commercial space travel, enabling individuals to experience space firsthand. Private companies are developing spacecraft and space tourism programs, creating a new market and expanding access to space.

Space Industry and Economy: The growing space industry fosters economic growth and job creation. It encompasses satellite manufacturing, launch services, space research and development, space tourism, and space-related technologies. The increasing participation of private companies and startups in space activities drives innovation and entrepreneurial opportunities.

Space Science and Research: Outer space exploration provides opportunities for scientific research and discovery. Missions to other planets, study of celestial bodies, and space-based experiments contribute to expanding our knowledge of the universe, technology development, and scientific advancements.

Space Mining and Resource Utilization: The concept of space mining involves extracting resources from celestial bodies, such as the Moon or asteroids, to meet future resource needs. This potential field could provide access to rare minerals, water, and other resources that can support space missions or be utilized on Earth.

Space Debris Management: As space activities increase, the management of space debris becomes crucial. Developing technologies and systems to track, mitigate, and clean up space debris present opportunities for innovation and sustainable space operations.

It's important to note that outer space activities also raise ethical, legal, and environmental considerations.

International cooperation, responsible governance, and adherence to space treaties and guidelines are crucial to ensure the sustainable and peaceful use of outer space for the benefit of humanity.

Could Space be where we develop a world with No Poverty, Zero Hunger, Good Health and Well Being, Quality Education, Gender Equality, Clean Water and Sanitation, Affordable and Clean Energy, Reduced Inequalities, Sustainable Cities and Communities, Responsible Consumption and Production, Climate Action, Peace, Justice, and Strong Institutions, and Partnerships for the Goals! A utopia living environment, created through Industry, Innovation, and Infrastructure for a new start for all mankind. But where?

Space, the final frontier! Through a joint effort, of the 178 countries that support the UNs' 17 SDGs, and capitalization on Industry, Innovation, and Infrastructure, we could create such a place. This is not a new idea, "in 1929 Hermann Noording developed the idea of a large wheel-shaped satellite reminiscent of the space station in the movie 2001: A Space Odyssey (1968).[9] It was a "...Princeton physicist Gerard K. O'Neill who saw huge orbiting communities as a means of salvation for Earth. Overcoming initial skepticism, he gained support from the National Aeronautics and Space Administration (NASA), organized a series of breakthrough workshops, and set forth detailed plans in his 1976 book The High Frontier."[9]

Solving Earth's problems in outer space. What it takes to build a great community in space?

Six tips developed:[10]

There Are Two Sides: Focus on creating a space that is welcoming for everybody. Be careful of being one-sided.

Neighborhood Watch: Think about your neighborhood; what's the best fit for your community? What does it need?

Community Assistance: Work with community members to help sculpt the direction of the space so you can create real impact on the surrounding community.

Gather: Provide interactive objects for people to gather around. i.e., dog parks, playgrounds, gardens, campfire/fire pits + more.

Power of The People: Give the people a say. Provide an opportunity for the community to have a say in some of the activities, classes, events, and happenings at the space.

Express Yourself: Think about creating a space that is both inspiring and allows everyone to express themselves. Think about other public spaces; what elements of those spaces bring people alive?

Utilizing the list of 17 SDGs, to create a space community through Industry, Innovation, and Infrastructure. A New World of Global Citizenship living in a self-contained Space Sustainable Cities and Communities. Through innovation and infrastructure developing a Utopia World.

Utopia World refers to an idealized or imagined society or world that is characterized by perfect or highly desirable qualities. The concept of Utopia has been explored by various philosophers, writers, and thinkers throughout history, envisioning a society that is free from social, political, and environmental issues. While Utopia is often seen as an unattainable ideal, it serves as a source of inspiration and a vision for a better future. Here are some key elements often associated with the concept of Utopia World:

Equality and Justice: Utopian societies typically prioritize equality and social justice. They aim to eliminate discrimination, poverty, and oppression, ensuring that all individuals have equal rights, opportunities, and access to resources.

Sustainable Environment: Utopian visions often prioritize environmental sustainability. They strive for harmony with nature, seeking to protect and preserve the natural world, while promoting sustainable practices and minimizing ecological damage.

Peace and Harmony: Utopian worlds are characterized by peace, harmony, and cooperation among individuals and communities. Conflict resolution, non-violence, and mutual respect are essential elements, fostering a sense of unity and collective well-being.

Education and Knowledge: Utopian societies emphasize the value of education and the pursuit of knowledge. They prioritize universal access to quality education, critical thinking, and intellectual growth, allowing individuals to reach their full potential and contribute to the betterment of society.

Freedom and Self-Expression: Utopias often uphold personal freedoms and respect for individual rights. They encourage self-expression, creativity, and diversity, fostering an environment where people can freely pursue their passions and ideas.

Health and Well-being: Utopian worlds prioritize the well-being of individuals, both physically and mentally. Access to healthcare, healthy food, recreational activities, and a balanced lifestyle are central to ensuring the overall well-being of the population.

Democratic Governance: Utopian societies often envision participatory and inclusive governance systems where decision-making power is distributed among the people. Direct democracy, consensus-based decision-making, and transparent institutions are commonly associated with Utopian ideals.

Through educated Global Citizens, develop a partnership with like goals, establishing a society of responsible consumption, and productions that does not interfere with the health and operations of a space community. A design that takes in account space pollution, while developing a climate-controlled environment for all. Life on land and below water, within the Space Community, free from contamination and pollution.

It's important to note that the concept of Utopia is subjective and can vary depending on cultural, social, and individual perspectives. While achieving a perfect Utopia may be unattainable, striving for a better world by working towards the values and principles associated with Utopia can lead to positive social change and progress.

But aren't we already contaminating and polluting Space with our trash? Space trash, also known as space debris or orbital debris, refers to the accumulation of man-made objects in Earth's orbit that no longer serve any useful purpose. These objects include defunct satellites, spent rocket stages, fragments from spacecraft, and other debris resulting from human space activities. Here are some key points about space trash:

Causes of Space Trash: Space debris is primarily caused by human activities in space, such as satellite launches, space missions, and intentional or accidental collisions between objects. These activities generate debris that remains in orbit, posing a risk to operational satellites and future space missions.

Impact and Risks: Space debris poses several risks and challenges. The high speeds at which debris travels in orbit can result in collisions that produce more debris. This phenomenon, known as the "Kessler Syndrome" or "collision cascade," could potentially render certain orbits unusable due to the high concentration of debris. Space debris also poses a threat to operational satellites, spacecraft, and the International Space Station (ISS). A collision with even a small piece of debris can cause significant damage or destruction.

Tracking and Monitoring: Space agencies and organizations around the world actively track and monitor space debris using radar, telescopes, and other detection systems. These efforts aim to catalog and predict the trajectories of known debris objects and provide warnings for potential collisions.

Mitigation Measures: To address the issue of space debris, mitigation measures are implemented to minimize the creation of new debris and reduce the risk of collisions. These measures include designing satellites and rockets to minimize fragmentation, using propulsion systems to deorbit spacecraft at the end of their missions, and adopting best practices for disposal of rocket stages.

Active Debris Removal: Various concepts and technologies are being developed to actively remove space debris from orbit. These include capturing and deorbiting debris, using nets, harpoons, or robotic arms to capture larger objects, or employing technologies such as lasers to modify the orbits of small debris.

International Cooperation: Space debris is a global concern, and international cooperation is essential to address this issue effectively. Space agencies, organizations, and governments collaborate on research, data sharing, policy development, and implementing mitigation measures to ensure the long-term sustainability of space activities.

Future Challenges: As space activities increase and more satellites are launched, managing space debris becomes even more crucial. The deployment of mega-constellations, such as satellite networks for broadband internet, poses new challenges in terms of debris mitigation and collision avoidance.

Efforts to address space debris focus on prevention, tracking, mitigation, and removal to ensure the sustainable use of outer space and protect critical space assets. Continued research, technological advancements, and international cooperation are vital to managing and reducing the risks associated with space debris.

WHAT CAN I DO NOW

Here are some ways that you and your community can take to contribute to a cleaner and more sustainable planet:

Reduce, Reuse, and Recycle: Practice the 3 R's to minimize waste. Reduce consumption by making mindful purchasing choices, reuse items when possible, and recycle materials that can be recycled.

Proper Waste Management: Dispose of waste responsibly by using designated recycling bins, composting organic waste, and properly disposing of hazardous materials. Avoid littering and participate in local clean-up events.

Conserve Resources: Conserve energy and water in your daily life. Turn off lights and appliances when not in use, use energy-efficient products, take shorter showers, and fix any water leaks.

Use Sustainable Transportation: Opt for walking, cycling, or using public transportation whenever possible to reduce carbon emissions. Carpooling and car-sharing services can also help reduce the number of vehicles on the road.

Support Renewable Energy: Invest in renewable energy sources like solar or wind power for your home if feasible. Advocate for renewable energy initiatives and policies in your community.

Choose Sustainable Products: Look for products with eco-friendly certifications, minimal packaging, and made from recycled materials. Support companies that prioritize sustainability and environmentally friendly practices.

Plant Trees and Native Plants: Trees play a crucial role in absorbing carbon dioxide and providing habitat for wildlife. Participate in tree-planting initiatives and consider planting native plants in your garden to support local ecosystems.

Advocate for Change: Raise awareness about environmental issues and advocate for sustainable practices in your community, schools, and workplaces. Engage in discussions, support environmental organizations, and participate in relevant campaigns.

Educate Yourself and Others: Stay informed about environmental challenges and solutions. Share your knowledge with others and encourage them to take positive actions for the planet.

Vote and Support Green Policies (when and where they make sense): Support political leaders and policies that prioritize environmental protection and sustainability. Vote for candidates who have strong environmental platforms and engage in environmental advocacy at local and national levels. Remember, even small actions can make a difference when multiplied by collective efforts. By adopting sustainable practices in our daily lives and spreading awareness, we can contribute to the cleanup and preservation of our planet for future generations.

While individual actions alone cannot solve complex global challenges, they are an integral part of the broader solution. When combined with collective efforts, policy changes, and systemic transformations, individual actions can make a meaningful difference in protecting our planet and creating a sustainable future for generations to come. Remember, individual actions, when combined with collective efforts, can make a significant impact. Encourage others to join you in taking steps towards a more sustainable

~ 49 ~

FINDINGS, SOLUTIONS, IMPLEMENTATION, CONCLUSION, AND RESPONSIBILITIES

FINDINGS:

The complexity of these issues is rooted deeper than one can imagine. Our planet is said to be more than 4.6 billion years old, and evidence exists that her health is in jeopardy. The jury has rendered a verdict, and humans are to blame for most of earths health issues. So how do we make Mother-Earth healthy again?

SOLUTIONS:

Innovation and technological progress are key to finding lasting solutions to both economic and environmental challenges, such as increased resource and energy-efficiency. Develop quality, reliable, sustainable, and resilient infrastructure, including regional and transborder infrastructure, to support economic development and human well-being, with a focus on affordable and equitable access for all. Promote inclusive and sustainable industrialization and, by 2030, significantly raise industry's share of employment and gross domestic product, in line with national circumstances, and double its share in least developed countries.

IMPLEMENTATION:

Implement enforceable regulatory requirements in all key areas. Establish inspection and evaluation criteria to be followed. Establish organization of single point of responsibility for providing the required research, development, and implementation of standards and evaluation. Change current policies of 2.8°C temperature rise by the end of the century to 1.5°C. This will help avoid irreversible and irreparable consequences.

CONCLUSION:

To improve the health of our planet, we must start at the lowest common dominator, humans! Think back to Iron Eyes Cody and his tears for what we have done to our planet, and what we continue to do. Like the narration said, "People start pollution, people can stop it!" We can each do our part. We can ensure that we are throwing out our trash in the designated disposal containers. Reduce the use of plastic products. Be smart consumers and minimize waste. Recycle! Incentivize recycling and reduce cost of accomplishing this process. Pressure local government to participate in these efforts. Be aware of our overall impact on these issues. It is our responsibility to our planet to act now.

RESPONSIBILITIES:

Saving the planet requires collective responsibility and action from individuals, communities, governments, businesses, and organizations. Here are some key responsibilities that contribute to efforts in addressing environmental challenges:

Individual Actions: Individuals play a crucial role in saving the planet through their everyday choices and behaviors. Responsibilities include practicing sustainable consumption, reducing waste, conserving energy and water, adopting eco-friendly transportation options, recycling and properly disposing of waste, and supporting environmentally responsible businesses.

Education and Awareness: Promoting environmental education and awareness is essential for fostering a sense of responsibility towards the planet. This includes educating oneself about environmental issues, sharing knowledge with others, and raising awareness through campaigns, events, and community initiatives.

Sustainable Practices in Businesses and Organizations: Businesses and organizations have a responsibility to adopt sustainable practices that minimize environmental impact. This includes implementing energy-efficient measures, reducing waste and emissions, adopting sustainable supply chain practices, promoting eco-friendly products and services, and integrating environmental considerations into decision-making processes.

Policy and Government Actions: Governments have a responsibility to develop and enforce policies that promote environmental protection and sustainability. This includes setting emissions reduction targets, promoting renewable energy, regulating pollution, conserving natural resources, and supporting sustainable practices through incentives, subsidies, and regulations.

International Cooperation: Addressing global environmental challenges requires international cooperation and collaboration. Countries need to work together to develop and implement global agreements and initiatives to tackle issues such as climate change, biodiversity loss, and pollution. Collaboration in areas like research, technology transfer, and financial assistance is also crucial.

Conservation and Restoration Efforts: Protecting

and restoring ecosystems, forests, and biodiversity is a shared responsibility. This includes supporting conservation initiatives, promoting sustainable land and resource management practices, preserving natural habitats, and taking steps to protect endangered species.

Sustainable Development: Balancing environmental protection with social and economic development is essential for long-term sustainability. Responsible development practices should prioritize the well-being of communities, ensure access to basic services, promote social equity, and integrate environmental considerations into development plans.

Advocacy and Activism: Individuals and organizations have a responsibility to advocate for policy changes, raise awareness, and mobilize action on environmental issues. This can include participating in protests, supporting environmental campaigns, engaging with policymakers, and amplifying the voices of marginalized communities affected by environmental challenges.

Saving the planet requires a collective effort, and everyone has a role to play. By recognizing our responsibilities and taking action in our personal lives, communities, businesses, and governments, we can contribute to a more sustainable future for our planet and future generations.

380 ~ JOHN H. SWINFORD III

$$\sim 50 \sim$$

MY OPINION

Much of the United Nation's SDGs sound very much like a socialistic approach which refers to the principles, policies, or systems that align with the ideology of socialism. Socialism is a political and economic philosophy advocating for the collective ownership and democratic control of the means of production, distribution, and exchange. It emphasizes social and economic equality, as well as the fair distribution of wealth and resources.

Historical experiences. There have been different historical examples of socialist systems, ranging from planned economies like the former Soviet Union to mixed-market economies with significant government intervention, like the Nordic countries. Supporters of socialism often point to successful social programs and policies in countries like Sweden and Denmark as examples of how socialism can work. But it is worth noting that even countries like Sweden and Denmark, that embrace elements of socialism, are still a mixed-market system where private enterprise coexists with government intervention.

I would argue that excessive government control and intervention can limit individual freedoms, stifle innovation, and lead to economic stagnation. Ronald Reagan once said, "If we look to the answer as to why for so many years we achieved so much, prospered as no other people on Earth, it was because here in this land we unleashed the energy and individual genius of man to a greater extent than has ever been done before."[3] He had also said, "The Founding Fathers knew a government can't control the economy without controlling people. And they knew when a government sets out to do that, it must use force and coercion to achieve its purpose."[3] Additionally, the potential for corruption and mismanagement can be a concern in centralized systems. Tell me one thing our government, here in the United States, manages within budget, in a timely manner, and that has customer satisfaction of the product or service being provided. I'll wait...because the real answer is, it is up to us to accomplish the requirements for a healthier planet, not our government.

REFERENCES

1. No Known Author (NKA). (1970). Keep America Beautiful: The Crying Indian in Canoe. Keep America Beautiful, Inc. Retrieved on 20 June 2023, from: https://www.youtube.com/watch?v=j7OHG7tHrNM.

2. No Known Author (NKA). (1970). Keep America Beautiful: The Crying Indian on Horse. Keep America Beautiful, Inc. Retrieved on 20 June 2023, from: https://www.youtube.com/watch?v=8_QGBWaD-A4.

3. Regan, R. (1981). Inaugural Address. Retrieved on 21 June 2023, from: https://www.reaganfoundation.org/media/128614/inaguration.pdf.

4. Schattle, H., and Lewin, R. (Ed.). (2009). The handbook of practice and research in study abroad: Higher education and the quest for global citizenship. Taylor & Francis Group. Retrieved on 19 February 2023, from: https://worldclassroom.webster.edu/courses/1431726/pages/week-3-overview?module_item_id=15452785.

5. UN. (2017). UN Chronicle. Global Citizenship. No. 4 Vol. United Nations. Retrieved on 19 February 2023, from: https://www.un.org/en/issue/374.

6. UN. (2023). 17 Sustainable Development Goals. United Nations, Department of Economic and Social Affairs Sustainable Development. United Nations. Retrieved on 19 February 2023, from: https://sdgs.un.org/goals.

7. Dewey, J. (2015) Democracy and Education on citizenship & education - excerpt.pdf. Retrieved on 26 January 2023, from: /courses/1431726/files/69320626/download.

8. Aristotle. Aristotle in 23 Volumes, Vol. 21, translated by H. Rackham. Cambridge, MA, Harvard University Press; London, William Heinemann Ltd. 1944. Retrieved on 26 January 2023, from: /courses/1431726/files/69320636?wrap=1.

9. Harrison, A. (2001). Communities in Space. CENGAGE. Encyclopedia.com. Retrieved on 03 March 2023, from: https://www.encyclopedia.com/science/news-wires-white-papers-and-books/communities-space.

10. Stanton, S. (2022). Building Community – 6 Tips to Creating a Great Community Space. Conscious Magazine LLC. Retrieved 03 March 2023, from: https://consciousmagazine.co/building-community/.